The Human Brain

The Human Brain

M. C. WITTROCK
Jackson Beatty
Joseph E. Bogen
Michael S. Gazzaniga
Harry J. Jerison
Stephen D. Krashen
Robert D. Nebes
Timothy J. Teyler

A SPECTRUM BOOK

PRENTICE-HALL, INC., *Englewood Cliffs, New Jersey 07632*

Library of Congress Cataloging in Publication Data
Main entry under title:

The Human brain.

    (A Spectrum Book)
    Includes bibliographies and index.
    1. Brain.   2. Learning, Psychology of.
I. Wittrock, Merlin C.   [DNLM: 1. Brain.
WL300 H9178]
QP376.H79   612'.82   77 8138
ISBN 0 13 444661 5
ISBN 0 13 444653 4   pbk.

A SPECTRUM BOOK

10   9   8   7   6

Printed in the United States of America

PRENTICE-HALL INTERNATIONAL, INC., *London*
PRENTICE-HALL OF AUSTRALIA PTY. LIMITED, *Sydney*
PRENTICE-HALL OF CANADA, LTD., *Toronto*
PRENTICE-HALL OF INDIA PRIVATE LIMITED, *New Delhi*
PRENTICE-HALL OF JAPAN, INC., *Tokyo*
PRENTICE-HALL OF SOUTHEAST ASIA PTE. LTD., *Singapore*
WHITEHALL BOOKS LIMITED, *Wellington, New Zealand*

Contents

v

III

Educational Implications of Recent Research on the Human Brain 131

Preface

Recent research into the structures and functions of the human brain has produced an impressive number of interesting and important findings about its operation. Newspapers and popular magazines occasionally summarize some of these important findings reported in scientific research journals. Neither news reports nor research articles, however, allow brain researchers to explain their latest findings to interested people who are unfamiliar with the technical vocabulary of the scientists. These interested people include teachers, school administrators, guidance counselors, undergraduate students—especially those in education and psychology—and lay people. This book provides these people with an opportunity to learn about recent research on the human brain.

In the following pages, several of the foremost researchers

on the human brain describe their recent findings. Dr. Timothy J. Teyler, an associate professor of neurobiology at Northeastern Ohio Universities College of Medicine, begins the volume with an illustrated introduction to the anatomy, chemistry, and physiology of the brain. He emphasizes the brain structures and functions, including arousal, motivation, learning, and memory, relevant to the interests of educators, students, and laypeople.

The second chapter, on the evolution of the brain, is written by Professor Harry J. Jerison of the University of California, Los Angeles, author of the highly regarded *Evolution of the Brain and Intelligence* (1973). Dr. Jerison presents an interesting description of how the human brain evolved to construct meaning and understanding from the complex sensory stimulation it continually receives.

The first of the three major sections of the volume, which deals with the fundamentals of the brain, concludes with a chapter by Dr. Jackson Beatty of the UCLA Brain Research Institute, who discusses the cognitive functions and processes of the brain, including the nature of consciousness, perception, sleep, dreaming, and decision making.

The second section delves into the hemispheric processes of the brain. In Chapter 4, Dr. Michael S. Gazzaniga of the State University of New York at Stony Brook, who is a pioneer in research on split brains, introduces and summarizes the recent interesting findings about the different processes of the right hemisphere and the left hemisphere.

Chapters 5 and 6 discuss research on the right and the left brain hemispheres, respectively. Dr. Robert D. Nebes, of the Duke University Medical Center, describes how the right or "minor" hemisphere characteristically organizes and processes information, including how it constructs wholes from partial sensory data. Dr. Stephen D. Krashen, a professor of linguistics at the University of Southern California, presents findings from research on the left hemisphere, including the ways it sequentially organizes information and understands and produces speech. He also discusses group and individual differences in brain processes, eye movements, and cognitive styles.

The final section of the volume, Chapters 7 and 8, deals with the educational implications of recent research on the human brain. Dr. Joseph E. Bogen, a neurosurgeon at the Ross-Loos Medical Group in Los Angeles, has performed many of the operations which led to the important findings about the hemispheric processes of the human brain. In Chapter 7 he discusses the implications for improving education which follow from an understanding of these processes.

I have written the eighth and final chapter, which is also on implications for changes in teaching methods and in the role of the learner in schools. Recent findings are used to build a new understanding of educational methods as they progressed from ancient Greece and Rome to modern times.

I wish to thank Dean John I. Goodlad of the UCLA Graduate School of Education and the University of California, Los Angeles for granting us permission to reproduce six of the following chapters, earlier versions of which originally appeared in the spring 1975 issue of the *UCLA Educator,* entitled "The Hemispheric Processes of the Brain": the chapters by Harry Jerison, Michael Gazzaniga, Robert Nebes, Stephen Krashen, Joseph Bogen, and myself. I am grateful to Sipora Gruskin for her editing of these six chapters, and to Lynne Lumsden and Carol Smith of Prentice-Hall for their editorial assistance on the entire manuscript. Finally, my thanks to Pat Zarell, who drew the illustrations in Chapter 1, and to Konrad Talbot, who prepared the Glossary.

—M. C. WITTROCK

The Human Brain

I

The Fundamental Processes and Structures of the Human Brain

1

An Introduction
to the Neurosciences

by Timothy J. Teyler

In our opening chapter, Dr. Timothy J. Teyler, an associate professor of neurobiology at Northeastern Ohio Universities College of Medicine, introduces the reader to the human brain's basic anatomical structures, chemical functions, and physiological functions. The illustrations in the chapter show the basic anatomical structures of the brain, the functions of the neurons, and the flow of information from sensory nerves to motor nerves. The text as well as the illustrations organize an incredible amount of information about the brain and its functioning in attention, arousal, motivation, learning, and memory. The chapter not only introduces concepts and ideas important to understanding information presented in later chapters, but, more importantly, presents a coherent and memorable explanation of the fundamental processes of the human brain as they are understood today.

What is the brain? The answer to this question depends upon who is asked. The anatomist, focusing on structure, may answer, "a collection of specialized cells, complexly arranged yet with commonalities." The physiologist, whose concern is processes, may answer, "an electrochemical mechanism that interacts with its environment and itself in particular ways." And the chemist perhaps says, "an incredible biochemical system specialized for the processing of information." To the nonprofessional, such as the reader of this book, the brain is rarely given much thought (although it is the source of all thought), but virtually everyone could agree that all human behavior is generated by the brain, to be expressed by muscles and glands, as well as all human thought, emotion, memory, and knowledge. The hypothetical answers above, from an anatomist, a physiologist, and a chemist, represent the three basic sciences upon which the brain sciences, or **neurosciences**,* rest. While individual scientists' goals differ, and all desire to know more of the workings of the brain, it is useful to remember that most scientists are interested in answering the following questions·

- What are the components of the brain, and how are they connected one to another?
- What are the functions of those components, and how do they work together?
- What are the chemical and electrical phenomena underlying the functioning of these components?

To certain nonprofessionals these are interesting questions today—and as more knowledge of the brain is gained, allowing man to manipulate the fabric of the brain, they will later become important questions to all. Knowledge of the workings of the brain is a potentially powerful tool to benefit mankind. The problems are waiting to be solved: mental retardation and mental illness, for example. But like most powerful tools, there also exists the potential for misuse. The ability to alter the fabric of the brain represents the application of a power more awesome than

*All the words that are boldfaced within the text are defined in the Glossary.

that contained in the nucleus of the atom. Only through education and awareness can this powerful tool be exploited for the benefit of mankind.

On a more pedestrian level, knowledge of the stuff of the brain may prove to be fascinating to many readers — the brain is, after all, responsible for all that we are and can become. To understand a bit of how the brain works is quite literally to gain insight into how man works.

The Brain

An examination of the surface of the human brain will show it to be a large (3 or more pounds), **bilaterally symmetrical**, wrinkled organ. The outer surface, or **cortex**, contains billions of brain cells (**neurons**) and the **processes** that connect one neuron to others. As we shall see, the cortex contains subdivisions with highly specialized functions. Toward the rear of the brain the **cerebellum** can be seen protruding from under the cortex. It, to, is a highly wrinkled, or **convoluted**, tissue concerned primarily with the coordination of commands to muscles. The convolutions of the brain's cortex represent an adaptation rendering more surface area available. The effect is similar to crumpling a piece of paper into a ball whose outer surface area is much less than the area of the paper itself. Since the major differences between the human brain and the brains of other mammals is in the number of neurons they possess and the interconnections among these neurons, the brains of related species — for example, of other primates — are similarly convoluted but to a lesser degree. Underlying the convoluted layer of cortical neurons are **tracts** of the fibrous processes (**axons**) that extend from and carry messages from cortical neurons to other neurons and vice versa. Examination of these fiber tracts with the unaided eye would show them to be relatively more white than the pinkish gray of the cortex. This is due to the fact that the lengthy axonal processes are often covered with a specialized insulating sheath of fatty tissue which appears white. This insulating sheath, termed the **myelin sheath,** serves to insulate one axon from its immediate surroundings and serves to speed its message-transmitting capacity by a factor of 10 or so. The process of **myelinization** is far from complete at birth, in some brain regions not being completed until puberty.

The cortical surface is not without regional distinctions. It is common to divide each hemisphere of the cortex into four **lobes** (Figure 1.1): from front to back, the **frontal, parietal, temporal,** and **occipital lobes,** each having somewhat different functions. All lobes, in man, can be divided into (1) zones that are either *sensory* or *motor,* and (2) zones that are termed *associational.* The **sensory zones** are areas for bodily sensations such as touch and temperature, and the **motor zones** are regions concerned with the control of muscular contractions. Sensory zones contain neurons that receive information from sensory organs and further process this information. Motor areas have neurons whose axons ultimately influence the musculature to produce movement. Although the cortex is only several millimeters thick, it contains a number of distinct layers in which are found: the **terminations** of information-bearing axons, output neurons, local processing neurons, and other, nonneuronal cells—the **glia.** The appearance of the layers under the microscope differs from one cortical zone to the next, with sensory zones having an expanded layer containing the terminations of information-bearing axons. Usually there are several separate zones for each sense, for example, in cats and monkey brains, the visual area contains three zones, the motor area two zones. In some cases we understand the functional differences of the various zones. For example, the three visual zones (termed V1, V2, and V3) contain neurons that respond to

BRAIN SURFACE

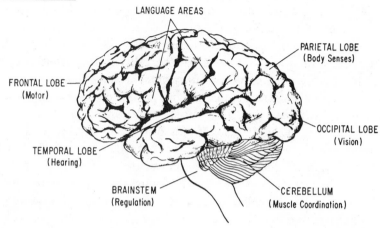

MIDLINE VIEW

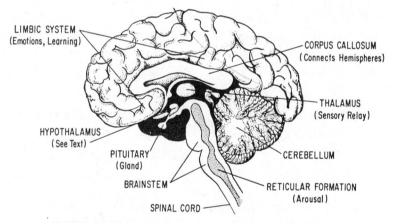

FIGURE 1.1. *Top:* The surface of the left hemisphere of the human brain with major areas and their functions labeled. *Bottom:* A midline view of the right hemisphere with the major areas/structures and their functions labeled.

different aspects of the visual scene, such as edges versus moving angles.

The **association zones** function as neither sensory analyzers nor motor programmers. In many cases we are almost totally ignorant of the precise function(s) of the association zones. In other cases we know them to be involved with, for example, the understanding of language or the perception of complex sensory information. A clue to their function comes from observations of the amount of association cortex in other species. Rats have a tiny amount, cats and dogs have much more, and cetaceans (whales and porpoises) come as close to the brain of man as do any. Since the amount of association cortex parallels the phylogenetic progression, and since the function of the association cortex for which we have clear information suggests a role in the more cognitive aspects of behavior, it is assumed that these functions are associated with the operation of association cortex. The increase in cognitive abilities across species nicely parallels the expansion of the association cortex. In short, it is probably association cortex that separates us from our fellow nonhuman creatures.

The cortical specializations found in each of the four lobes are as follows (in addition each lobe of the human brain contains association cortex):

- *Frontal lobe:* motor areas for all of the skeletal muscles in the body; cells in these zones send axons to neurons in other parts of the brain as well as long axons (3 feet in man, 30 feet in the blue whale) to neurons in the spinal cord which, in turn, send axons directly to muscles.

- *Parietal lobe:* bodily sense areas receiving axon projections from other brain areas (**subcortical** areas) whose function is to process and pass on body sense information gained from **receptors** located in the skin, joints, and other tissue.

- *Temporal lobe:* auditory sense areas receiving information indirectly from the **cochlea** of the ear. There are multiple auditory analyzers in the temporal lobe, each probably dealing with a different aspect of the auditory world.

- *Occipital lobe:* cortical sensory analyzers for information from the retina of the eye.

A large bundle of fibers, the **corpus callosum,** serves to connect the two **cortical hemispheres.**

The registration of sensory information on cortical neurons is not a simple one-to-one affair. There are numerous subcortical "relay" areas that do not simply relay the information but process it at each stage in its journey from receptor to cortical receiving area. In addition, there is a considerable degree of *convergence*, a coming together of various signals to a single point, and *divergence*, the radiating of a signal to many points. These seemingly contradictory processes work together in the processing of information by the brain. As information about the sensory world ascends through the processing stations of the brain on its way to the cortical receiving areas, the signal, while changed, does not lose its form or pattern. Take, for instance, the registration of a moving spot of light on the retina, analogous to viewing an illuminated table tennis ball in a darkened room. A certain portion of the retina is activated and neural impulses stream toward the brain. As the optic fibers terminate on their subcortical relay station in the thalamus, they form a "pattern" of the retina in the **thalamus.** Similarly, the fibers going from the thalamus to terminate in the visual cortex of the occipital lobe retain the pattern of the retina. Thus the spot of retina activated by light from the illuminated ball is represented on the visual cortex by a spot of activated cortical tissue. This general rule holds for all sensory projections—they project to the cortex (and intermediate relay stations) such that the surface of the receptor (retina, skin, cochlea) is mapped out on the surface of the cortex. The mapping is, however, quite distorted, although all parts are present. In the bodily senses of touch and temperature the distortion is such that in man the fingers, lips, and tongue are grossly out of proportion, being much larger than would be the case with a one-to-one mapping. The reason for this apparent distortion is that the brain allocates cortical space not by surface area but by receptor density. Humans have the highest density of skin receptors in the fingers, lips, and tongue. The bodily sense cortical projections of a house cat would have a grossly large area devoted to the sensory receptors supplying the whiskers of the face and a relatively small paw representation. At each stage of sensory processing, there are neurons that respond to specific aspects of the stimulus — its shape, color, or movement. These neurons, often responding to only a tiny fragment of the whole stimulus, are termed *feature extractors*. The aspect of a stimulus they respond to appears to be genetically determined but can be altered by changing the environment.

Underlying the cortex are a virtual panoply of subcortical brain structures — most of which we will conveniently ignore. For our purposes we have adopted the convention of dividing the central nervous system into four parts: the **forebrain,** of which the cortex is a part; the **midbrain;** the **brainstem;** and the **spinal cord.** The changes across phylogeny that were mentioned earlier are by and large limited to the forebrain. The midbrain, brainstem, and spinal cord are little changed across a wide range of species. The **thalamus,** a forebrain tissue, as we have seen acts to process and relay visual information to the cortex. For this purpose it has a specialized collection of neurons, known as a **nucleus,** to accomplish this task. In fact, the thalamus, as the major sensory relay in the brain, contains relay nuclei for each of the senses. In addition, it possesses other nuclei specialized for other jobs — such as widespread activation of the cortical association areas, a function presumably linked to **arousal** processes. Mammals deprived of sensory cortex due to a genetic accident or surgical removal experience only the crudest aspects of sensory experience, such as intensity and frequency; the fine patterning of the sensory world is unavailable to them.

The other forebrain structure of interest to us is not a single nucleus, nor even a collected group of nuclei, but rather a physically widespread yet closely interconnected group of structures known collectively as the **limbic system.** The names of some of the structures are intriguing: *amygdala, hippocampus, septum.* Equally as intriguing and mystifying to neuroscientists is the function of the limbic system. Humans deprived of the hippocampus, through surgery to control epilepsy, suffer an inability to store events into permanent memory. Animals apparently do not share this deficit but display a diverse symptomology which has spawned many theories as to hippocampal function ranging from a role in inhibiting behaviors that are no longer relevant, to keeping track of objects in space. We simply do not know the function of this brain area.

The midbrain—located, not surprisingly, in the middle of the brain—is made up of the **reticular formation** and the **hypothalamus/pituitary**. Running up through the base of the brain and ending in the midbrain is a diffuse structure known as the *reticular formation* (Figure 1.2). This core of neural tissue

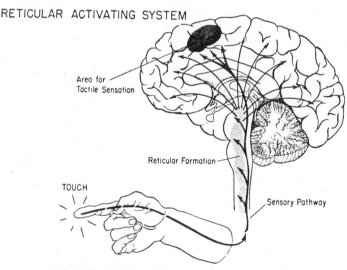

FIGURE 1.2. The reticular activating system. Incoming sensory information from touch receptors on the finger is fed into the reticular formation (stippled area). The reticular formation activates the entire cortex by means of a widespread fiber system. The touch information is relayed by the thalamus to the cortical area for tactile information (shaded area).

receives sensory information en route to the thalamus and cortex. Unlike the thalamus, its fibers do not project to circumscribed areas of the cortex—rather, they are widespread and have diffuse connections with many brain regions. Electrical stimulation of the reticular formation in a sleeping animal will awaken the animal—suggesting a role in arousal. This is confirmed by experiments in which the reticular formation was rendered inactive, producing a continual somnolent state, and by noting that sedative drugs act at this location. Some of the neurons in this area have incredibly long projections, with thousands of connections established throughout the brain—further attesting to the widespread nature of reticular formation effects.

If a case could be made for one "brain center," the only viable candidate would have to be the *hypothalamus*, a nuclear structure located above the roof of the mouth in man. The reasons for choosing the hypothalamus as a brain area of major importance are as follows: it has widespread connections with many other brain areas; it is intimately connected with the master **endocrine gland**—the pituitary; and it has been found to be involved in a wide variety of behaviors and processes. Since whole books the size of this one could be, and have been, written on the hypothalamus, we shall again summarize. The hypothalamus has one overriding duty—the maintenance of relatively constant internal conditions, termed **homeostasis.**

The body is not unlike an incredibly complex factory wherein separate assembly lines must be coordinated such that the output meets the demand of the marketplace—if demand increases, this information must be "fed back" to the assembly lines to enable them to produce more. So, too, the hypothalamus regulates many activities by the judicious application of "feedback." Such behaviors as eating and drinking, and such physiological functions as temperature regulation and reproduction, are largely governed by the hypothalamus. We will briefly examine one system governed by the hypothalamus in order to appreciate its function and how it executes that function. Drinking water is vitally important, as most organisms cannot store appreciable amounts of water. There is a limited range of water levels within the body; any excess water is excreted, any deficit brings into play water-seeking behaviors (the sensation of "thirst" and the behaviors undertaken to alleviate the sensation). Sensors are located in various parts of the body: stretch receptors in the vessel walls of the **cardiovascular system** which signal a loss in blood, and thus water volume; **osmoreceptors** in the hypothalamus that respond to changes in the salinity (degrees of saltiness) of body fluids (with dehydration the salinity of body fluids increases); chemical receptors in the hypothalamus that detect the presence of a chemical (the hormone angiotensin) secreted by the kidney under low-body-water conditions; and sensory receptors in the mouth, which, surprisingly, play a minor role in the regulation of thirst. All of this information is sent to the hypothalamus, where it is "interpreted" and decisions made as to the appropriate response.

The means that the hypothalamus has at its disposal to implement its decisions are several. The hypothalamus can manufacture a hormone (**antidiuretic hormone, ADH**) and store it in the pituitary to be released upon a neural command from the hypothalamus. ADH acts upon the kidney to reduce the excretion (elimination) of water in the urine. It does this by causing the kidney to "recycle" body water and thus produce concentrated urine. In addition, the hypothalamus is presumably involved in the sensation of thirst (and the converse, satiation) and the water-seeking behaviors that accompany it—although the means by which the rest of the brain interacts with the hypothalamus in this behavior is by no means fully understood.

The hypothalamus is intimately connected to the *pituitary* by a slender stalk. The two tissues work in concert; in fact, the division between brain and gland is somewhat arbitrary. To give an idea of the "**holistic**" nature of the brain/gland system, consider that in many situations the gland is driven into activity (and secretes a hormone into the blood) by a "local hormone" released by the hypothalamus. The pituitary hormone causes activity elsewhere (for example, the **gonads**) and, in turn, the secretion of gonadal hormone into the blood, where it is sensed by the hypothalamus. Thus the hypothalamus is provided with information regarding the "effectiveness" of its action and is in a position to increase or decrease the output of its "local hormone." This principle of control is seen in many everyday situations — for example, in adjusting the flow of water out of a lawn sprinkler. Your hand (hypothalamus) turns on the faucet ("local hormone") and you adjust the flow depending upon the area covered by the sprinkler (circulating levels of target-gland hormone).

Proceeding further down into the brain, we are confronted with a portion of the brain that has least changed across species — the *brainstem*. Many brain nuclei and nerve tracts exiting from **higher brain centers** and incoming sensory fibers are found here. In addition, this area contains nuclei of the **autonomic nervous system** — a relatively involuntary division of the nervous system that **innervates** the **visceral** organs, vessels, and **ducted glands**. The autonomic nervous system has two divisions: **sympathetic** — increasing its activity in times of stress or arousal; and **parasympathetic** — relatively more active during quieter times. Most organs are supplied with nerves from both divisions of the autonomic nervous system. Nuclei concerned with motor control are located in the brainstem. Although technically not considered a brainstem structure, the *cerebellum* communicates with the rest of the brain via the brainstem and is involved in the control and cooperation of muscles and muscle ensemblages.

The last structure on our quick anatomical tour is the *spinal cord* — whose diameter in man is the size of your little finger — which contains ascending and descending nerve tracts, large neurons (**motorneurons**) whose job it is to induce muscular contraction, and smaller neurons whose job, in part, is to contribute to motor control and facilitate **reflexive behavior**.

Much can be gained by examining the brains of different species and the developing brain of a single species. Figure 1.3 graphically depicts a phylogenetic comparison across several

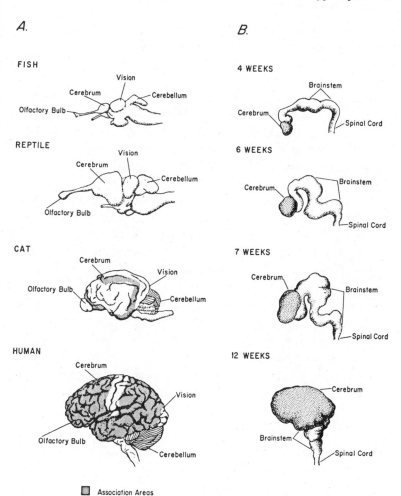

FIGURE 1.3. *A.* A comparative view of brain anatomy. The drawings of the brains of fish through man are not to scale. Note the diminished predominance of the **olfactory** bulb and the tremendous increase in the size of the cerebrum. Association cortex is absent in fish and reptiles and is fully elaborated in the human brain.

B. The development of the human brain in the first four to twelve weeks of life. The basic structure is established at twelve weeks, with cell division and brain growth proceeding rapidly up to the time of birth.

species (*A*) and the **ontogenetic** development of the human brain (*B*). Phylogenetically, the brainstem is very similar across species whereas there are marked differences in the forebrain. The growth of the forebrain, particularly the cortex, is evident. Since the basic unit of the brain, the neuron, is similar across a wide phylogenetic span, man's dominant status in large part must rest upon his tremendous cortical endowment—rivaled only by the whales and dolphins. Note the shaded cortical areas; they represent association cortex in which the phylogenetic disparity is even more pronounced.

Across ontogeny the brain differentiates out of a mass of neuron precursors, the **neuroblasts**. Cell division proceeds at a rapid rate such that the basic architecture of the brain is complete at birth, to be modified and expanded in its subsequent environment. Out of a primitive neural tube, the forebrain, midbrain, and brainstem rapidly emerge to form identifiable structures even at the earliest ages. Cell division is occurring at a furious pace (doubling every few days in some instances) in contrast to the absence of cell division soon after birth. All the while neurons are migrating about in the embryonic brain to eventually assume their final and correct locations—an awesome phenomenon that has remained a mystery for years.

The Neuron

The basic unit of the brain is the neuron. Anywhere from 20 billion to 200 billion neurons encompass the brain of man at birth. Surprisingly, we never have more neurons than when we are born—we lose thousands daily, never to be replaced, and apparently not missed until the cumulative loss builds up in very old age (and even then not all individuals are affected similarly). Each of these neurons communicates with as many as a thousand other neurons making the total number of connections and the "wiring diagram" very complex indeed. Neurons are very similar across species, although the neurons of lower organisms communicate with one another primarily by "electrical" contacts between neurons and those of higher organisms (particularly the vertebrates) communicate primarily by "chemical" contacts (to be discussed below). As can be seen in Figure 1.4, neurons come in a variety of shapes and sizes, some with one or two processes extending from the cell body of the neuron, others with richly branching processes resembling a tree in winter.

A neuron is like other cells of the body in that it possesses a continuous cell membrane enclosing the **cytoplasm**. Neurons have a cell nucleus and the **metabolic** machinery necessary to maintain life. In addition they are specialized for the integration and transmission of information. A prototype neuron is shown in Figure 1.4. The short, branching processes extending from the cell body are **dendrites** (known collectively as the **dendritic tree**). These processes receive information from other neurons. The long process is the **axon**, which is often covered with the myelin sheath. Information is transmitted along the length of the axon, which ends at another neuron or a muscle. The neuron has a normal "direction" of operation: information comes in at the region of the dendrites, and the results of a neuron's processing is sent out via the axon. The **synapse** refers to the region of communication between two neurons (or between neuron and muscle). In the electrical synapses of lower organisms, the membranes of the two communicating neurons are tightly fused and the information from neuron A influences neuron B by an electrical process. The chemical synapses of higher organisms are somewhat different. The axon membrane of neuron A does not physically touch the dendrite of neuron B; instead, there is a tiny gap (about 1/50,000,000 of a meter) between them—the **synaptic gap**. When information arrives at the axon terminal of neuron A, a small amount of a chemical substance (termed the **neurotransmitter**) is released from the axon terminal and diffuses across the

THE NEURON

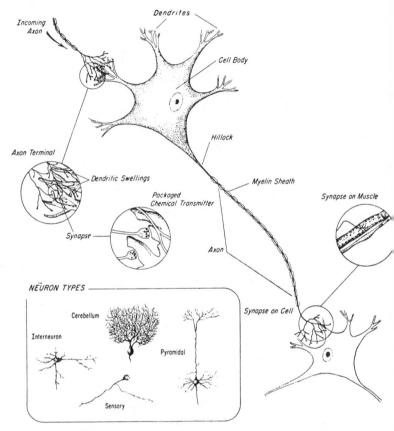

FIGURE 1.4. The neuron. A prototype neuron showing its processes and communication (synapse) with other neurons and with muscle. *Inset:* Several of the types of neurons encountered in various parts of the brain.

synaptic gap to influence the dendrites of neuron B. Synapses are often found on small swellings of the dendrite. The influence of the neurotransmitter can be to either arouse (excite) or depress (inhibit) the activity of neuron B. The neurotransmitter is stored in tiny packages inside the axon terminal (Figure 1.5) and is released in sufficient amounts only when its neuron is active.

THE SYNAPSE

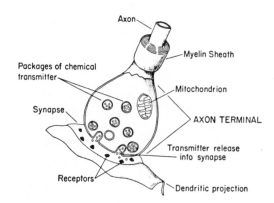

RESTING NEURON

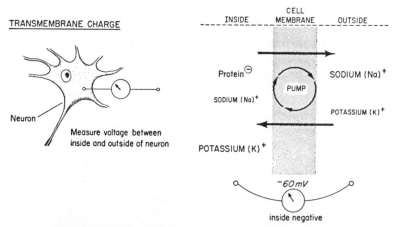

FIGURE 1.5. The synapse. *Top:* Cutaway view of an axon terminal showing the packaged transmitter chemical and the synaptic region. *Bottom:* Features of the resting neuron showing the transmembrane charge (left) and the unequal distribution of charged molecules and ions due to the Na^+/K^+ pump (right).

What causes the release of the packaged transmitter? To answer this question we must examine how a neuron becomes "active." The membrane of a neuron is like a sieve, allowing the passage of small molecules and charged atoms (**ions**) from one side of the membrane to the other, but preventing the movement of larger molecules and ions. In addition, the membrane contains a "pump" that expels positively charged sodium ions (Na^+) and takes in similarly charged potassium ions (K^+). The net result of the leaky membrane, the Na^+/K^+ pump, and the presence of negatively charged protein molecules inside the cell is an **electrical potential** (imbalance) between the interior and exterior of the neuron. The potential is such that the interior is negative with respect to the exterior.

A nonactive or resting neuron displays a potential (termed the **transmembrane potential**) of about -60 millivolts. If the transmembrane potential is lowered (made less negative) to about -50 millivolts, the neuron will initiate an "**action potential**" in its axon. The action potential is a momentary opening of minute "gates" in the axon membrane, first allowing Na^+ ions to rush into the axon and then allowing K^+ ions to rush out. An electrode measuring the transmembrane charge during an action potential would see an abrupt swing from the resting level of -60 millivolts to approximately $+10$ or 20 millivolts due to the inflow of the positively charged Na ions. The subsequent elimination of the positively charged K ions results in a return (and brief negative overshoot) to the resting level (see Figure 1.6). One of the functions of the Na^+/K^+ pump is to redress the ionic imbalance brought about by the ion flow during an action potential.

The action potential begins at the hillock of the axon and travels down the axon at speeds up to 300 feet per second. This is slow compared to the velocity of a purely electrical potential (186,000 miles per second—the speed of light) and is due to the fact that while electrical potentials are associated with an action potential, the phenomenon itself is a time-consuming process involving the opening and closing of ion gates and the flowing of ions through the membrane gates. When the action potential arrives at the axon terminals, it causes the release of some of the packaged neurotransmitter. The transmitter diffuses across the synaptic gap to attach to receptor sites on the membrane of the dendrites. There it has an excitatory or inhibitory effect on the recipient cell.

An action potential is initiated, as mentioned, by lowering the transmembrane charge; this comes about through the action of excitatory neurotransmitters at the synapse.

Excitatory neurotransmitters lower the transmembrane charge toward the action potential threshold, while inhibitory neurotransmitters raise (make more negative) the transmembrane charge. The dendritic synapses are some distance away from the hillock of the axon, the site of action potential initiation, and their contribution is diminished as a function of distance. Rarely is the activity of a single synaptic contact sufficient to trigger an action potential (or **spike**). Thus several excitatory synaptic inputs must be active more or less simultaneously (within milliseconds) to raise the transmembrane charge to threshold and fire a spike. In contrast, an active inhibitory synapse on one portion of a dendrite can counteract the effect of an active excitatory synapse on an adjacent portion of the dendritic tree. These properties are depicted graphically in Figure 1.6. A neuron has hundreds or thousands of synapses, many of which are active at any given time. The transmembrane charge, and thus the initiation of a spike, is dependent on the net synaptic influence on a neuron. More excitatory input relative to inhibitory input will trigger a spike; more inhibition than excitation will not.

Synapses in the brain are the primary site for intercellular communication—yet any individual synapse is not a "secure" communication channel. The ability of a single synapse on a typical neuron to produce an action potential depends upon many factors, such as: the type of neurotransmitter (excitatory or inhibitory); the transmembrane charge as influenced by prior activity on other synapses; the amount of neurotransmitter released; the distance of the synapse from the action potential trigger zone in the axon hillock; the simultaneous activity of other synapses on the recipient cell; and the past history of the synapse (many synapses are altered by their prior "experience" and are said to be "plastic"—a characteristic presumably present in synapses that play a role in behavioral learning). An analogy can be drawn to a political demonstration. When many individuals are shouting different slogans at the same time, it is difficult to

---

THE ACTION POTENTIAL

FIGURE 1.6. The action potential. *Top:* Expanded view of a section of axon showing a "snapshot" of an action potential traveling down the axon. Opening of submicroscopic gates in the axon allows the passage of ions in the direction indicated by the arrows. The ion movement and altered transmembrane charge they produce constitute the action potential. *Right:* Upon arriving at an axon terminal, the action potential causes the release of a neurotransmitter into the synapse. Synapses are either excitatory or inhibitory depending upon the neurotransmitter chemical released and the properties of the receptor. Shown in the graphs are the effects of weak and strong activation of an excitatory synapse (top) and an inhibitory synapse (middle). Prior to stimulation, the recipient neuron is at resting level (− 60 mV). After the neurotransmitter reaches the receptors on the recipient neuron (allowing time for the action potential to traverse the axon), it causes the transmembrane charge to go toward **spike threshold** for excitatory synapses and to go away from spike threshold for inhibitory synapses. Strong stimulation of the excitatory synapse will result in an action potential in the recipient cell. When both excitatory and inhibitory synapses are activated (as is normally the case), their effects algebraically sum. This is shown in the bottom graph where the dashed lines indicate the contribution of the excitatory and inhibitory synapses and the solid line represents their sum and thus their influence on the recipient cell.

understand the message. In this setting information is best communicated either by shouting in unison or by silence on the part of the crowd while listening to a spokesperson.

In summary, a neuron will release neurotransmitter from its axon terminals provided that its synaptic excitation exceeds its synaptic inhibition sufficient to reach spike threshold. In one sense a neuron behaves like a hybrid computer: analog operating characteristics in the dendritic tree, digital operating characteristics in the axon. The reader should be warned that, for brevity and clarity, the whole story is not presented here. Unfortunately for

THE SYNAPTIC POTENTIAL

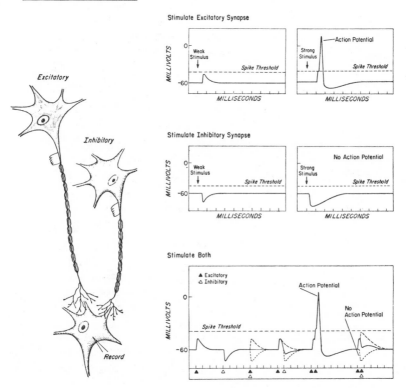

neuroscientists interested in unraveling the complexities of the brain, all neurons are not as simple as has been outlined above. To provide only two examples: some neurons are capable of generating spikes on their own dendritic trees and some synapses are *reciprocal* (information can pass in both directions).

What are the neurotransmitters and why are they important? The scientific criteria for establishing the identity of a synaptic neurotransmitter are exceedingly stringent. To date, only one neurotransmitter has been completely identified in the **central nervous system** — **acetylcholine**, an excitatory transmitter at the skeletal nerve-muscle junction. Acetycholine has also been identified in the cortex and thalamus by **assaying** for the presence of the enzyme that inactivates the neurotransmitter. Other neurotransmitters in the brain and their areas of localization have not been definitively identified, although substantial evidence exists concerning their roles as neurotransmitters:

- *Dopamine*: an inhibitory transmitter found in subcortical motor nuclei and in limbic system connections to the cortex. This candidate neurotransmitter, a **catecholamine**, has been linked to Parkinson's disease, a condition characterized by a pronounced muscular tremor. The disease is associated with a degeneration in the major dopamine nucleus — the **substantia nigra**. Dopamine itself, if injected or ingested, would not gain entry into the brain, being blocked by a system of protective barriers known as the **blood-brain barrier**. Dopamine has also been linked to mental illness by the observation that the most effective antipsychotic pharmaceutical agents act by blocking dopamine synaptic transmission (sometimes giving rise to "Parkinson"-like side effects).

- *Norepinephrine*: one synthetic step beyond dopamine (both are obtained from dietary **phenylalanine**) is the inhibitory neurotransmitter norepinephrine. A region of the brainstem, the **locus coeruleus,** is a major source of the widely projecting norepinephrine nerve fibers. These fibers project to the cortex, limbic system, hypothalamus, spinal cord, and elsewhere.

- *Serotonin*: an inhibitory neurotransmitter that has been implicated in cognitive functions, mental illness, and sleep cycles. The cell bodies of serotonin-releasing fibers are found in the **raphé nuclei** of the brainstem. One of the drugs of abuse of the 1960s and early 1970s, LSD, bears striking chemical similarities to this neurotransmitter.

Several other suspected neurotransmitters have been discovered, and more are sure to come. It is possible that the various specialized brain "circuits" each possess a unique neurotransmitter. The study of the "chemical anatomy" of the brain is expected to answer this and many other questions.

The brain, as we have seen, is an electrochemical machine. Not surprisingly, it can be altered in its function by the addition of "foreign" chemicals. Many drugs have little or no central nervous system action, primarily because they are prevented access to the brain by the blood-brain barrier. Those that do gain access interact with various processes in the brain. *Alcohol*, for example, is a central nervous system depressant and is similar in action to the **barbiturates.** While the precise mechanism of action of this drug is being actively investigated, it is not improbable that it acts by interfering with brain metabolism or acts at the ion gates referred to above. The effect of alcohol and the barbiturates, which were or are used as general anesthetics, is also observed with the administration of certain paint thinners, glue, and industrial solvents that contain benzene, toluene and xylene. These agents are powerful brain depressants and, when abused, can lead to serious complications or death.

Other drugs are central nervous system excitants. Examples

129070

include the **amphetamines** Methedrine, Dexedrine, and Benzedrine. These drugs, too, have been subject to much abuse. Their mechanism of action in the brain appears to involve the facilitated release of packaged neurotransmitter from axon terminals such that neural excitability is increased due to the elevated synaptic concentration of the transmitters. When abused, these agents are particularly dangerous as addiction develops, and heavy use can lead to the development of both a drug-induced psychosis and deterioration of brain tissue.

The **narcotics**, especially those derivatives of opium such as heroin, are technically **analgesics** in that they alter the perception of pain. The property leading to their abuse, however, is the euphoria associated with the drug. These agents are addicting. Their mechanism of operation is being pursued; it appears that they activate certain naturally occurring receptors on neurons to produce their effect. Once their mechanism of action is known, we may be able to prevent or treat drug addiction more effectively than at present.

Several drugs are rather similar in chemical structure to naturally occurring neurotransmitters and have a powerful effect on awareness and perception. Among these **psychotomimetic** drugs are: mescaline (derived from the peyote cactus)—structure similar to one of the catecholamines; LSD—structure similar to serotonin; and marijuana—a mild psychotomimetic that does not have structural similarities to any known neurotransmitters. Aside from their chemical similarities to neurotransmitters, their mechanism of action is not known.

Brain Processes

Our knowledge of brain processes is most complete when considering sensory functions or motor control—we know relatively little of brain processes associated with thinking, reasoning, motivation, and other of these more "cognitive" processes. An examination of known brain processes may provide us with an understanding of general principles of brain functioning. These general principles may also prove to hold for cognitive processes of which we have only fragmentary knowledge today.

Earlier in this chapter we have seen that the analysis of sensory events by the brain operates by a principle of feature extraction. As sensory information is relayed through the brain, neurons respond to particular aspects of the stimulus, some coding aspects of patterning, some coding movement, and some coding other aspects such as color or musical pitch. An example of feature extraction in the visual cortex of cats is seen in Figure 1.7. It is easy to conceive of how such an analyzer could work, but

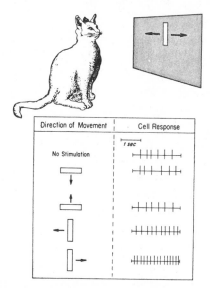

FIGURE 1.7. Feature extraction. An electrode capable of detecting the activity of a single neuron in the visual cortex has been painlessly implanted in the cat's brain. The cat watches a bar of light move across a screen. Simultaneously, the activity of the neuron is recorded—each vertical line represents an action potential. This cell is most responsive to a movement to the right, as shown by its discharge rate.

very difficult to understand how the result of this analysis is entered into our conscious awareness of the world.

We have also seen that feedback is an important aspect of brain functioning. Without feedback control we would experience difficulty performing even the simplest act. We are able to stand upright without falling over only by integrating the various relevant signals and adjusting the musculature appropriately. The brain is a very efficient integrator of information. In this example, information from pressure receptors on the feet and in the **semicircular canals** of the ear's **vestibular system**, as well as visual information, are analyzed. Given perturbation of the system (e.g., a gust of wind), similar information would be registered in several sensors and the appropriate correction made. The system can be confused by providing discrepant information to the sensors. An example of the latter is the "tilting room" of a fun house in which a perfectly level room visually appears to be tilted. In this case the visual input is at odds with the other sources of information. The brain integrates this discrepant visual information with the other sources—the result is that people adjust their bodies to compromise the discrepant information from the various sensors. So too do we compromise our cognitive responses to sources of disparate information. Children confronted with diverse reactions to their inappropriate behavior may not be able to determine what behavior patterns are desired and, as a consequence, may select a behavioral solution that represents a compromise to the conflicting demands. If the reactions are too diverse, causing the feedback loop to fail, the reactions will be ineffective in modifying the child's behavior—with unfortunate results. So too in the tilting room example; if the information is too discrepant, an individual will simply fall down—a failure of feedback control due to conflicting information input.

Learning implies a relatively permanent alteration in behavior as a result of experience. It also implies the relatively permanent storage of the results of learning. The search for brain **correlates** of learning and memory is confounded by the existence of an apparent paradox. The electrical stimulation of discreet areas of the brain in unanesthetized neurosurgical patients often results in vivid memories of past events, some of which were apparently "forgotten" by the patient. This suggests two things. One, the brain has an infinite capacity for memory, although it may not always be possible to retrieve certain memories. Indeed, no one has ever "filled up" the brain with memories such that further remembering is impossible. Second, it would appear that there exist discreet locations where memory is stored. Herein lies the apparent paradox. Experiments with animals wherein portions of the brain were surgically removed indicated that specific memories were *not* deleted. Rather, the degree of behavioral deficit was related to the *amount* of tissue removed rather than its specific *location*. Thus, on the one hand it appears that memories are localized, while on the other hand they appear to be diffuse. While these experiments have been criticized on a number of grounds, the paradox remains. The hypothetical memory trace is often referred to as the **engram**. The search for the engram has been approached in a variety of ways. One of the most promising involves recording the activity of neurons throughout the brain in an animal with permanently implanted electrodes while the animal is learning a task. These experiments have shown that while there are some areas that seem particularly involved with the learning process (for example, the hippocampus) and some areas that are apparently not involved, many areas of the brain do show neural changes associated with behavioral learning. It is therefore possible that the engram has no discreet location but is represented by a diffuse and perhaps redundant network of altered neurons.

The nature of the alteration in the brain as a result of information storage is unknown. This is not to say that potential mechanisms have not been proposed and examined — they have. Among them are: changes in neuronal **RNA** and protein, changes in the amount of transmitter released, growth of new synaptic contacts, and changes in the physical/chemical properties of the synapse. In some simple systems (**invertebrates**), the synaptic mechanism responsible for **decrementing** synaptic transmission (*habituation*) has been delineated; it involves a decrease in transmitter release from axon terminals. This finding may have important implications, since habituation is a universal phenomena involving the elimination of responding to a meaningless stimulus. It is by no means certain that all neurons will be found to employ the same mechanism of change. Ultimately we may understand these mechanisms and be in a position to modify their processes — thus modifying the ability of an organism to learn and remember.

The process of converting a learned behavior into a relatively permanent engram has been found to be a time-dependent process. When a behavior has been learned, it is susceptible to interruption for a brief period of time, thus preventing its "consolidation" into an enduring engram. This is the period of **short-term memory**. Amnesia following a **trauma** to the brain is a common occurrence in accident victims and is also seen following psychiatric electroshock therapy. These persons cannot remember events immediately preceding the trauma. Once consolidated into *long-term storage*, memories are no longer affected by these treatments, which primarily modify the ionic properties of the neuron membrane. **Long-term memory** can be disrupted by treatments that inhibit the systhesis of proteins (structural proteins are presumably involved in any enduring engram). Thus it is thought that memory consolidation involves two phases: (1) a transient change in the neural membrane, and (2) a relatively enduring structural change of the neuron. There are documented cases of individuals incapable of forming long-term memory engrams. These persons, who suffer from damage to the hippocampus and midbrain structures, can learn normally and have intact short-term memory, but are incapable of long-term storage (or retrieval).

A defining characteristic of the human species is the presence of a formal language. Research has delineated two regions on the "dominant" hemisphere (usually the left hemisphere for right-handed individuals) specialized for language. They are **Broca's area** in the frontal lobe and **Wernicke's area** in the temporal lobe. Damage to Broca's area due to injury or stroke results in a person incapable of producing smooth, well-articulated speech — although the content and meaning are normal. Damage to Wernicke's area results in well-articulated speech almost totally devoid of content. These observations, and others, have led to the notion that Broca's area is primarily concerned with language production whereas Wernicke's area is primarily concerned with **semantic** (meaning) aspects of language.

Much of what we learn are **motor skills**. Riding a bicycle, typing, operating machinery, and playing the piano are highly skilled motor behaviors. The acquisition and retention of motor skills are somewhat different than more cognitive skills. Once acquired they appear to endure for long periods of time even in the absence of practice. They often occur with such rapidity as to question if each movement is consciously directed, as in the playing of an experienced pianist. The hippocampal-damaged patient referred to earlier, suffering from a lack of long-term memory, has no trouble remembering newly learned motor skills for long periods of time. Yet he is unable to *verbally* report any recollection of the skill or of how to perform it.

The fabric of the brain is set down as a result of the inter-action of genetic blueprints and environmental influences. While the basic features of brain organization are present at birth (cell division is essentially complete), the brain experiences tremendous growth in neural processes, synapse formation, and myelin sheath formation, declining around puberty. These processes can be profoundly altered by the organism's environment. Rats reared in an enriched environment (with litter mates in a cage full of "interesting" objects) show marked changes in brain development as compared to rats reared in impoverished environments. Furthermore, it has been shown that brain processes present at birth will degenerate if the environmental stimulation necessary to activate them is withheld. It appears that the genetic contribution provides a framework which, if not used, will disappear, but which is capable of further development given the optimal environmental stimulation. The social and political implications of this fact of brain functioning are obvious and far-reaching.

To those being introduced to the neurosciences it is often informative to outline the pattern of information flow in the brain. While this cannot be done with complete confidence, it is illustrative of the regions activated by a simple sensory and motor event. In Figure 1.8 the information flow resulting from touch receptors on the finger is diagramed. On the top is the sensory registration of the event relayed from the thalamus to the parietal lobe, accompanied by widespread reticular formation activation of the cortex. In this depiction, the event is being cognitively evaluated by the frontal association cortex to result in the issuance of a motor command (Figure 1.8, bottom) to move the hand and finger. The motor output originates in the frontal motor area, is further modulated by subcortical motor areas and the cerebellum, and projects into the spinal cord to terminate on motor neurons projecting to the appropriate muscles (not shown). The reader will appreciate that many relevant brain areas involved in this simple stimulus-response mechanism have been omitted for clarity. Even for this elementary behavior, widespread areas of the brain are engaged.

The measurement of brain activity is a limiting factor in our understanding of its function. The limitations are imposed due to the technical limitations of the procedure and to the intrusive effects of the recording device on the normal operation of the brain. In human beings the only widely used means of directly measuring brain activity is through the use of scalp electrodes. These electrodes measure the summed activity of millions of neurons lying under the skull. When the neurons are **synchronously** active, the resultant record (the **electroencephalogram, EEG**) shows rhythmic waves of various frequencies. When the neurons are *asynchronously* active, the EEG becomes less rhythmic. An analogy can be drawn to a crowd of people on a basketball court.

INFORMATION FLOW IN THE BRAIN

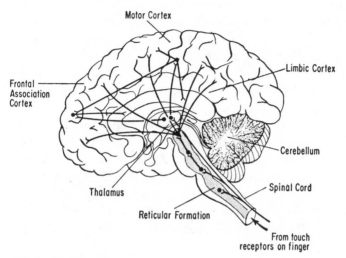

SENSORY CORTEX : Input

Motor Cortex

Limbic Cortex

Frontal
Association
Cortex

Cerebellum

Thalamus

Spinal Cord

Reticular Formation

From touch
receptors on finger

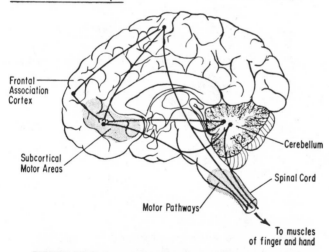

MOTOR CORTEX : Output

Frontal
Association
Cortex

Cerebellum

Subcortical
Motor Areas

Spinal Cord

Motor Pathways

To muscles
of finger and hand

FIGURE 1.8. Information flow in the brain. *Top:* Brain areas activated by sensory information from touch receptors on the finger. *Bottom:* Brain areas involved in the isssuance of motor commands to muscles of the finger and hand. In the interest of legibility, many brain areas involved in this simple situation are not shown.

When they all jump up and down in concert, the floor rebounds up and down in large swings. When the individuals in the crowd each jump independently, the undulations of the floor are smaller and of higher frequency. Since the EEG records the activity of a large population of neurons, it is not particularly valuable for examining the fine tuning of the brain. It has proved of use in measuring the general state of arousal of an individual, as is shown in Figure 1.9.

The most precise information regarding neural activity comes from recording the activity of single neurons, particularly with electrodes that are capable of penetrating the cell membrane to detect the transmembrane charge. While this provides a great deal of information about neural processing, it is technically difficult and faces the rather nasty problem of sampling the activity of a very few cells out of the billions in the brain. These

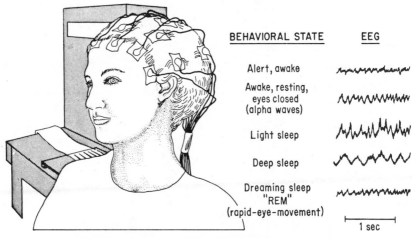

FIGURE 1.9. The electroencephalogram (EEG). Scalp electrodes can measure the activity of large populations of neurons. When the neurons act in synchrony, waves can be recorded— for example, alpha waves—associated with relaxed wakefulness. Particular EEG patterns are associated with certain behavioral states, as is depicted here.

recording techniques are intrusive and are not normally used in examining human brain functioning.

In summary, the brain is an incredibly complex electro-chemical machine. The neurosciences are still in their infancy but are progressing rapidly in uncovering the mysteries of the brain. We do know that it is an exquisitely built tissue capable of being modified, for good or bad, by its environment. It is not altogether ridiculous to drawn an analogy between the brain and the United States, in which the citizens represent neurons and cities represent nuclei. Cities are connected by lines of communi-cation and often perform specific duties—for example, commerce, tourism, manufacturing. Individuals in the cities work at those duties and influence other individuals, but few are really indis-pensable. The sum of society's knowledge (memory) is distributed throughout the citizenry. And finally, the country is influenced, for good and bad, by its environment—both natural and man-made.

*   *   *

*Suggestions for
Further Reading*

GENERAL

GAZZINGA, M. S. & BLAKEMORE, C. *Handbook of psychobiology.* New York: Academic Press, 1975.

Chapters devoted to current research areas; assumes an introductory knowledge of the brain.

KUFFLER, S. W., & NICHOLLS, J. G. *From neuron to brain.* Sunderland, Mass.: Sinauer, 1976.

A high-level book emphasizing mechanisms of neural operations.

ROSENZWEIG, M. R., & BENNETT, E. L. *Neural mechanisms of learning and memory.* Cambridge: MIT Press, 1976.

Chapters devoted to current research on brain processes of learning and memory in man and animals; assumes an introductory knowledge of the brain.

TEYLER, T. J. *Brain and Learning.* Stamford, Conn.: Greylock, 1978. Chapters contributed by leading researchers into the biological bases of learning and memory; assumes an introductory understanding of the brain.

TEYLER, T. J. *A primer of psychobiology.* San Francisco: Freeman, 1975.

An elementary introduction to the brain; assumes no background.

THOMPSON, R. F. *Introduction to psysiological psychology.* New York: Harper & Row, 1975.

A college-level textbook; broad coverage of brain and behavior.

NEUROANATOMY

BRODAL, A. *Neurological anatomy* (2nd ed.). New York: Oxford University Press, 1969.

A high-level anatomy text that does an admirable job of integrating structure and function.

GARDNER, E. *Fundamentals of neurology* (6th ed.). Philadelphia: Saunders, 1975.

An integrated presentation of brain anatomy and physiology, moderately advanced.

NOBACK, C. R., & DEMAREST, R. J. *The nervous system: Introduction and review.* New York: McGraw-Hill, 1972.

An easy-to-read, well-illustrated beginning book on brain anatomy.

NEUROPHYSIOLOGY

ECCLES, J. C. *The understanding of the brain.* New York: McGraw-Hill, 1973.

An intermediate-level text with sections on brain development and cognitive functions.

KANDEL, E. R. *Cellular basis of behavior.* San Francisco: Freeman, 1976.

KATZ, B. *Nerve, muscle, and synapse.* New York: McGraw-Hill, 1966.
A fairly difficult book dealing with the biophysics of neural function.

SCHMIDT, R. F. *Fundamentals of neurophysiology.* New York: Springer-Verlag, 1975.
An intermediate-level textbook with emphasis on motor, sensory, and homeostatic systems.

NEUROCHEMISTRY

COOPER, J. R.; BLOOM, F. E.; & ROTH, R. H. *The biochemical basis of neuropharmacology* (2nd ed.). New York: Oxford University Press, 1974.
A difficult but comprehensive book on the biochemistry of the brain and synaptic transmission.

JULIEN, R. M. *A primer of drug action.* San Francisco: Freeman, 1975.
An introduction to the chemistry of the brain and the effect of drugs on the brain.

2

Evolution of the Brain
by Harry J. Jerison

Dr. Harry J. Jerison, a professor of psychiatry and psychology at UCLA and a member of the Mental Retardation Research Center, explains how our brains and our minds have evolved. He presents an intriguing explanation of the evolutionary development of language as a supersensory system that originally contributed to imagery—to our capacity to imagine—rather than to communication. From the evolution of our brains, he develops an explanation of how our minds have evolved to construct an inner real world which we use to explain the massive amount of information we receive and transmit.

Biological systems can always be analyzed most interestingly by beginning with their evolutionary history. It is, therefore, appropriate to introduce research on the human brain with a review of the actual history of the brain as an organ of the body. My review begins with a discussion of the present status of evolution as a biological topic, emphasizing evidence about the evolution of the brain. Since the discussion, later, is on **encephalization** and relative brain size, the second section of this chapter is a discussion of the meaning of these aspects of the brain, followed by a brief section on misconceptions about brain evolution. The longer sections that follow review our present knowledge of the evolution of encephalization and its implication for our understanding of the evolution of mind and intelligence.

The Scientific Status of Evolution

There are facts about evolution and there is theory. Many of the facts of the evolution of the brain are revealed in the fossil record. One need merely examine the **endocasts** made from the cranial cavities of fossil animals of different groups and from different geological levels to see some of the most important facts about how the brain evolved. Numerical methods help us to see these facts and are theoretical only in the sense that addition and subtraction are theoretical.

It is a fact, for example, that the relative size of the brain in hooved and carnivorous mammals has increased and become diversified as these major groups of mammals evolved during the past 50 million years (Jerison, 1976a). It is a fact that the complexity of certain external features of the brains of dogs and their relatives has increased during the past 30 million years (Radinsky, 1973). And it is also a fact that the **hominid** brain has approximately tripled in size during the geologically brief evolutionary span of the past 1.5 to 4.5 million years (Tobias, 1971). These are examples of the facts of evolution about which there can be questions only with respect to methods of measurement and definition.

There is, of course, theory in the study of evolution, and one can legitimately argue the claims of various theories that have been advocated by biologists in recent years. The theories are not idle speculations but involve rigorous analysis without which the facts would be difficult to interpret. The best of the present theories are highly mathematical, such as Fisher's (1930) and Lewontin's (1974). All modern theories are Darwinian. They recognize that Darwin's first great achievement was to present the facts of evolution so clearly that no educated person could reject them. Darwin's second great achievement was his theoretical statement about the role of **natural selection**, which has since been verified in many experimental studies (Dobzhansky, 1970). There are differences among current theories with respect to the emphasis on natural selection as opposed to roles for genetic drift and other factors, but no theory questions the basic facts of evolution, which are much better known and understood today than they were in Darwin's time.

The theoretical approach to evolution as presented in this chapter follows Simpson's (1953) analysis, which is the one most suited for a broad view of the data from the fossil record. Simpson (1964) has also presented the clearest statement of the nature of evolutionary evidence—fact and theory—for an educator who might be required to review it when facing a local school board or regional boards of education. I do not raise this last issue lightly. It is here that some of the most significant interactions between science and society occur and where difficult problems have arisen (Grabiner & Miller, 1974). One of the issues is about the place of facts in one's world of beliefs, a philosophical question especially relevant for the analysis of evolution.

The distinctions between fact and theory are more subtle than one usually supposes. Precise statements of facts often depend on the theories used for their analysis and the theoretical framework within which facts are discovered. These issues can usually be neglected by scientists because of the broad consensus that appears in most productive scientific fields. Such consensus about the proper paradigms for one's work, so ably discussed by Kuhn (1970), is a necessary part of science, but it is well for both the practitioners and the critics to be aware of its role. My own view is somewhat closer to Karl Popper's (1972) in believing that many of the facts of science, in particular the evolutionary facts discussed in this chapter, are invariant under the transformation of one's paradigms. In other words, I believe that they are true in the everyday sense; their "truth" does not depend on one's philosophical framework. This is certainly so for the simple facts that I will present because those facts are derived from the size and shape of the cranial cavity of fossil animals. The changes in those sizes and shapes are the incontrovertible facts of the evolution of the brain.

Significance of Size and Shape of the Brain

The fossil evidence is limited to external features visible only on the outer surface of the brain and is available from the endocasts of fossil animals. Endocasts are casts for which the cranial cavity acts as the mold, and are remarkably brainlike in appearance in almost all birds and mammals. Less brainlike for lower **vertebrates** (fish, amphibians, and reptiles) in which the brain does not usually fill the cranial cavity completely, the endocasts usually provide at least a general picture of the surface features of the brain and can almost always be used to estimate brain volume.

I earlier reviewed the matter in detail (Jerison, 1973) and presented several hypotheses about the evolution of mind in vertebrates to explain some of the facts. These hypotheses will be summarized here as important implications of the organic evolution of the brain for issues in education and human behavior. The general hypothesis is that the mind or intelligence resulted from natural selection for encephalization, which is defined as the evolution of larger brains beyond the enlargement that could be predicted from the evolution of larger bodies. The facts of the evolution of the brain, specifically of the evolution of encephalization, are thus the basis for a theory of the evolution of mind or intelligence (Lashley, 1949; Jerison, 1976a). The theory refers to differences among species, of course, and not to the variation in brain size (or intelligence) within a single species.

The formal theory requires, first, some understanding of the significance of size per se in studies of the brains of different species. It is now reasonably well established (Jerison, 1973, Chapter 3) that differences in gross brain size in different species of mammals are strongly correlated with numerous microscopic characteristics of the brain as a whole. Some of these are the total number of nerve cells in the cerebral cortex, the concentration of acetylcholine (an important chemical for transmitting nerve impulses from one neuron to another) in the cortex, the total amount of cortex, the ratio of neurons to glial cells, and the size of various subcortical structures in the brain. These correlations are rarely below .95, and in some instances they are very nearly 1.0. The significance of such high (nearly perfect) correlations is that if one knows how much the brain of a mammal weighs, one can estimate with reasonable accuracy the number of cortical neurons in that brain and the various other structural and chemical features of the brain just discussed.

These facts are the basis of a theory of encephalization and brain size in which various comparisons among species with respect to intelligence are proposed (Jerison, 1973, 1977). Although there has been interest in such comparisons since Darwin's time (e.g., Huxley, 1863, Darwin, 1871), appropriate behavioral tests have been difficult to devise. The theory has suggested certain unsuspected groupings, which can be tested by observations of behavior. Among the primates, the gibbons, which are species of small apes, are grouped with rhesus monkeys and cebus monkeys and below the great apes such as orangs, chimpanzees, and gorillas, with respect to behavioral capacity or intelligence. On the other hand, the baboons, though close relatives of rhesus monkeys, are placed above all other monkeys and intermediate between monkeys and great apes. These groupings are consistent with observations of behavior in the primate species (Hodos, 1970).

The approach just described refers to between-species differences. It cannot be applied in a simple way to within-species effects such as variability of human brain size, because there is little or no relation between brain size and intelligence in living human beings (Mettler, 1956; Tobias, 1970). The issue is superficially perplexing because it implies that between-species variations and within-species variations in the brain result from different mechanisms. Interestingly enough, this is exactly the distinction that is made in the theoretical analysis of evolutionary phenomena. According to such analysis, most of the genetic variation producing the within-species effect is probably of a type (nonadditive) that is not affected by natural selection. The same kind of analysis suggests that some aspects of intelligence as measured by IQ tests, which also show an unusual degree of variability in human populations, may be different from the kind of intelligence that evolved when the hominid brain was going through the genetically determined increase in size as we evolved during the past 3 million years or so. The theoretical basis of the analysis is in the application of Fisher's (1930) "fundamental theorem of natural selection," which is discussed by Falconer (1966), by McClearn and De Fries (1973), and in somewhat different terms by Lewontin (1974).

There is also a fossil record of the changes in the shape of the brain. This record is usually considered in connection with the evolution of the pattern of convolutions, the **gyri** and **suli** that give a brain its characteristic appearance in textbook illustrations. I do not emphasize these data because of the poor representation of fissures in fossil hominid endocasts. There is some controversy on this matter; one author (Holloway, 1974) reads significance into certain aspects of the appearance of hominid endocasts to help decide when the speech areas developed. The present consensus, however, would agree with von Bonin's (1963) position, discounting such interpretations as permitting little more than questionable speculations. There is evidence of **asymmetry** in a Neanderthal endocast which supports the evolution of language areas in the brains of these early representatives of *Homo sapiens* (Le May & Culebras, 1972), but the appearance of a possible third frontal convolution in other hominid brains is not sufficient evidence for a language area (Jerison, 1975).

There is actually no need for controversy about this issue. The important question is about the evolution of language as a hominid **adaptation**. Here the best evidence comes from the use of an evolutionary principle that is not based on the meager fossil record of hominid endocasts. This important principle is the "uniformitarian" hypothesis (Simpson, 1970) as enunciated by Lyell, the great geologist who was Darwin's mentor, critic, and friend. The proposition is that present forces acting in the universe have always acted in more or less the same way. Applied to the brain, the proposition is that the organization of the brain in a species today reflects a development from a similar organization in species ancestral to it. The most notable of the species-specific behaviors of living species should, therefore, have been foreshadowed in their ancestors. Language and linguistic behavior are traits which characterize us as a living species of vertebrates, and it is inconceivable that such central traits should have developed from scratch in man. From the extensive neural representation of language in the human brain and from the uniqueness of this aspect of our structure as vertebrates, one would be inclined to identify the evolutionary enlargement of the hominid brain with the evolution of language. One would not necessarily assert that language was associated with a particular stage of that evolution (although such an assertion would not be unreasonable), but one would consider the unusual aspects of the endocasts of fossil hominids as compared to fossil apes to be related to the evolution of that most peculiarly human of hominid features: speech and language. Since so much of the size of the human brain can be associated with the cognitive aspects of human behavior, especially those related directly or indirectly to language, the increase in size in the endocasts of fossil hominids may be associated with the development of comparable adaptations or **preadaptations** (Jerison, 1976b).

SOME MISAPPREHENSIONS
ABOUT BRAIN EVOLUTION

In nonprofessional (and some professional) conversations about the evolution of the brain one may hear, "It's not the size of the brain that counts, rather it's the complexity of the convolutions." In more neurologically sophisticated groups it might be, "It's not the number of neurons in the brain, rather it's the complexity of their interconnections." To achieve a better sense of what is and is not important, let me comment, briefly, on the issues underlying such statements.

With respect to the convolutional pattern, there is no complete consensus at this time, but my own observations have led me to accept a principle first stated by Baillarger (1853) and developed by LeGros Clark (1945): the degree of convolutedness in a brain is due to its gross size. Large brains tend to be convoluted, whereas small brains tend to be smooth. These are between-species comparisons, that is, comparing large-brained and small-brained species rather than comparing individuals of the same species. Within a species the degree of convolutedness is approximately constant, regardless of size. Measurements of the degree of convolutedness of brains are, therefore, equivalent to those of brain size. They add no new information for the analysis of complexity of organization or behavioral capacity.

A somewhat different set of questions must be considered when relating the number of neurons in the brain to the complexity of the interconnections. It can be shown by quantitative methods that as the total number of neurons increases, the degree of connectivity must increase, and both are simple functions of brain size (Jerison, 1973). In this sense, brain size is a natural biological statistic that can be used to estimate other biological features of the brain, including the degree of convolutedness, the number of neurons, and the complexity of their interconnections. Since most characterizations of intelligence consider exactly such **parameters** when defining intelligence in biological terms (Butcher, 1968), the relationship between brain size and intelligence (in the between-species sense) is understandable.

The misapprehensions about the role of brain size and of the features related to brain size can be avoided if we distinguish gross brain size from a fraction or component associated with body size and another fraction or component associated with encephalization. Most of the evolutionary increase in brain size should be understood in exactly the same terms as the evolutionary increase in the size of the liver, heart, and other organs of the body. During the past 60 million years there was a major diversification with respect to body size in the evolution of the mammals. This diversification of body size accounts for most of the variation in brain size in living mammals. Only about 20 percent of the variance in brain size is explained as resulting from encephalization, the increase that is not the result of the body size factor. It is encephalization that may be correlated with the evolution of biological intelligence. It is this 20 percent that interests us most because it explains much of the superiority of the higher primates (monkeys and apes) over most other mammals with respect to behavioral measures. And it is this 20 percent that accounts for the fact that the human species (like the dolphins) has a brain that is about 6 times as large as that of an average living mammal. The remainder of this chapter is devoted to the history of encephalization and its interpretation as the basis of the evolution of mind.

Evolution of Encephalization

There are clues in the present diversity of vertebrates and the 500 million years of their evolution that enable us to make significant conjectures about the significance of encephalization. I must refer you to my monograph for a complete analysis (Jerison, 1973) and to other reports (Jerison, 1975, 1977) for more recent information, but the important facts are these:

- Of the 40,000 or so identified species of living vertebrates, the majority are lower vertebrates, and there is little or no evidence of encephalization in any of these. The lower vertebrates include fish, amphibians, and reptiles, and a total of about 25,000 to 30,000 species have been described. Although their brains differ considerably in the patterns of adaptations, which are revealed in regional enlargement for behavioral specialization, the total mass of brain tissue in almost all is significantly below that of higher vertebrates. (The interesting exceptions include some sharks and dinosaurs.) This has always been true as far as one can tell from studies of relative brain size in fossil fish, amphibians, and reptiles, including most dinosaurs. There is an important conclusion to be drawn from this fact: many structures other than the brain must contribute to successful adaptations to **environmental niches**. Vertebrates do not live by brains alone.

- The earliest known bird, the 150-million-year-old *Archaeopteryx*, already had a brain slightly larger than those of comparable reptiles though smaller than that of the smallest-brained living bird of its body size. It was truly a missing link with respect to its brain, just as it was in other respects (Ostrom, 1974). The most interesting aspect of the evolution of the birds is that although they are obviously higher vertebrates with respect to encephalization, their encephalization was not clearly related to the evolution of "intelligence" as one would normally use that term. With respect to versatility, modifiability, or plasticity of brain and behavior, it is only by unusual laboratory procedures, quite unnatural for the normal life of birds, that one can demonstrate that birds are comparable to mammals with respect to "behavioral capacity" (Lashley, 1949; Thorpe, 1956). The direction of behavioral evolution in birds has been to perfect in extraordinary ways the **fixed-action pattern** as a behavioral mode, although as one learns more about the neural control of such patterns, it becomes more and more clear that these are normally developed through an interaction between genetically determined "programs" and the experience of the bird during its early development (Hinde, 1969).

- The earliest mammals appeared about 200 million years ago and the history of the mammalian brain is known as of about 150 million years ago. The details of mammalian history are of central importance to the understanding of the evolution of intelligence, and the points that I would emphasize are these:

Although they were more encephalized than reptiles throughout their early history, the mammals were stable with respect to the size of their brains (relative to body size) for their first 100–150 million years. Their brains were then about 20 percent the size of living mammals but about 4 times the size of reptilian brains. This means that the early mammals must have found a stable niche in the world of their time with respect to the demands on the brain.

During the past 50 million years or so, almost all groups of mammals (the opossums may be the only exception) showed some tendency toward further encephalization. In most instances the present level of encephalization was achieved early in the evolution of each group and then maintained for the remainder of the group's history. This was true for insectivores (moles, shrews, hedgehogs, etc.) and prosimians (primitive primates such as lemurs) which achieved their present levels about 40 or 50 million years ago; it was also true of the highly encephalized whales and dolphins, which reached their present levels about 20 million years ago.

The primates have always been more encephalized than the typical mammals of their time, throughout their long history. (Primates are among the earliest known orders of living mammals—older than rodents or horses, for example). Thus, primates of 40 or 50 million years ago, though smaller-brained than their living descendants, were 2 to 4 times as encephalized as their contemporaries among other groups of mammals.

The major evolutionary enlargement of the hominid brain, which began about 3 million years ago and culminated about 250,000 years ago with the evolution of the true human brain in *Homo sapiens,* was a unique phenomenon in its time. No other group of vertebrates showed any evidence of brain enlargement during their evolutionary history of the past 3 million years. (It is appropriate for popular comparisons of man and dolphin to note the different rates of evolution of encephalization in these two groups. The dolphins were at their present level of encephalization for about 20 million years, whereas the human species did not achieve its present level until a fraction of a million years ago.)

Evolution of Mind

We are almost ready to use the facts just reviewed to reconstruct a possible evolutionary history for mind. But we first have to note a few **morphological** facts about the way neural tissue is packed in the visual, auditory, and olfactory systems.

The neural system for vision includes extensive networks in which millions of nerve cells are packed in the retina of the eye rather than in the brain. These are known to be involved in such complex neural analysis that the retina might legitimately be characterized as a brain lying outside the cranial cavity (Sherrington, 1950). Other sensory systems do not have this characteristic. The reptiles, from which mammals evolved, have only a few hundred nerve cells in the auditory system external to the brain, and although they have more olfactory cells external to the brain, these are not involved in integrative activity but are specialized for one-way transmission of unanalyzed information to structures within the cranial cavity.

The puzzle that led to the first conjecture about the evolution of mind was the early encephalization followed by the unusually long period of stability in the evolution of the mammalian brain. Why did the early mammals show encephalization in the first place? And why did encephalization then stay at the archaic grade until over 100 million years later in the history of the mammals? The answer must have been that the mammals discovered a new niche for vertebrate life; by characterizing that niche we will answer our questions.

We must begin with some prehistory of encephalization evident in the prior history of reptiles on earth, and we must recognize that the earliest mammals were essentially specialized reptiles. Prior to the appearance of true mammals the major land vertebrates were the mammallike reptiles (synapsids) which were the dominant reptiles until about 230 million years ago at the end of the Paleozoic era, although the earliest ruling reptiles (archosaurs) had already appeared. One characteristic of all reptiles at that time was undoubtedly that they lived by day, using excellent reptilian vision (still characteristic of most reptiles; see Polyak, 1957) as their basic source of information about distant events. The fossil record shows that the ruling reptiles (such as dinosaurs) and the mammallike reptiles were in competition for the normal reptilian niches and that the ruling reptiles won the competition early in the Mesozoic era or "Age of Reptiles." The mammallike reptile species all became extinct by the middle of the Age of Reptiles, although they survive (in a sense) in one lineage we have come to call "mammals."

The secret of the evolution of certain mammallike reptile species into true mammals was, I submit, that they found a set of niches in which they did not have to compete with ruling reptiles. These were niches for "nocturnal reptiles" that could be normal with respect to their ability to use information about events at a distance, but had to be peculiar in that they could analyze those events by using nonvisual distance senses, namely audition (hearing) and olfaction (smell). It is here that we see reasons for the expansion of the brain in such "reptiles" which are now known to have been the earliest mammals.

If audition and olfaction are to be used in a way analogous to vision, millions of neurons must be added to those systems. Those would be neurons doing work analogous to the work of retinal neurons in a normal reptile. But there is no room near the peripheral sense organs for hearing or smell to pack those extra neurons. (In the case of olfaction the pathway already leads into the brain proper and it would have to reverse itself to package extra neurons external to the brain.) If those sensory systems were to expand to be useful as sources of information about events at a distance, the brain would have had to expand to contain the additional neurons. According to this analysis, the first expansion of the mammalian brain had nothing to do with intelligence. It was merely the solution to a packaging problem of where to put the extra nerve cells of the auditory and olfactory systems of a nocturnal animal.

BEGINNINGS OF CONSCIOUSNESS

If we reconstruct the experiences of an early mammal as a nocturnal "reptile" that used audition and olfaction as well as vision as distance senses, we will see consciousness as selectively advantageous. We must recognize, first, that the amount of information processed by a vertebrate nervous system is enormous and that there must be considerable encoding of information, analogous to encoding subroutines in computer programs. A spatial code is inherent in the structure of the visual system, beginning with the retina and continuing in the brain. It is a map of what one sees, with every point named, as if it were a street address. This is the spatial code, and the names are spatial labels. A temporal code, with time-labels, is inherent in the environmental stimuli and in the physiology of the auditory system. It is a system that works mainly with information involving time, though it can translate that into information about space, as in the use of sonar-like echolocation by bats and whales and in the common capacity to localize the source of a sound. The encoding of olfactory information remains pretty much a mystery: the dimensions of the stimulus are still not well understood and it is difficult to discover a code when the nature of the information to be encoded is uncertain. But olfactory information transformed into information about events at a distance must be given some spatial code. In any event, it is clear that with the evolution of elaborate auditory and olfactory systems in the brain, space and time had to be encoded in some sense. We may think of the evolution of such systems in the early mammals as preadaptive for providing roles of space and time as dimensions of a real world.

The earliest mammals, though assumed to be nocturnal, must still have received some distance information through their visual systems (adapted for night vision as in most living mammals), and this information would have to be integrated with that from the auditory and olfactory channels. There would be need to verify it by comparing it with information from proximal senses, including the tactile senses, and to integrate it also with sensory feedback from the motor system if the animal moved. The meaning of integration and verification here is that a code must be established to indicate when different kinds of neural in formation refer to the same environmental source or event, and the obvious form of that code would be to label the source as an "object."

In these paragraphs I have developed the concepts of space, time, and object as creations (codes or subroutines) of the nervous system. This, it seems to me, is a fundamental way of looking at the work of the brain. We might describe it as creating a real world. Reality is, thus, a creation of the brain, a model of a possible world that makes sense of the mass of information that reaches us through our various sensory (including motor feedback) systems.

All animals with sufficiently large brains (perhaps all vertebrates, but certainly all birds and mammals) create their various real worlds according to this evolutionary analysis, although those worlds will differ from one another just as the brains that create them differ (von Uexküll, 1934). This would be as true for us and our perception of reality—the real world that we experience—as it is for any other animal.

HUMAN CONSCIOUSNESS

Man is special because we have evolved what might be termed a supersensory system. This is the system of speech and language which has many similarities to other sensory and motor systems but also has some peculiarities. Among the peculiarities, for example, is the fact that the language systems of the brain are not represented bilaterally, certainly not to the same extent as are the true sensory systems of the brain. This is an unexplained exception to the normal symmetry of neural functions (Teuber, 1974). Among the similarities to sensory systems, the important role of environmental factors for normal language development may provide the most interesting example because mammalian sensory systems must be used in appropriate environments to develop normally (Blakemore, 1974). It is a major **nature-nurture interaction.**

The most difficult aspect of the analysis of the evolution of speech and language is to understand the selection pressures on early hominids that resulted in this unusual adaptation. The issue is not solved, but I will conclude this chapter with a speculative analysis of what may have happened (cf. Jerison, 1977). The first proposition is that language did not evolve as a communication system, although that may be its primary function as we know it today. From an evolutionary point of view, the initial evolution of language is more likely to have been as a supplement to other sensory systems for the construction of a real world. This would be consistent with the other evolutionary changes in mammalian neural adaptations and would not require the sudden appearance of an evolutionary novelty. The suggestion is that our ancestors evolved a more **corticalized** auditory sense that was coupled with the use of vocal capacities for which almost all living primates are notorious.

Why would such a system evolve in early hominids? The answer can begin with the presently conventional view of the early hominid niche as that of a broad-ranging, social, predacious, ground-dwelling primate species. The niche is somewhat comparable to that of the baboons, which have been the most frequently chosen sources of information about how early hominids might have lived, or to that of the great apes, which are forest animals, though these primates are not basically predacious. A more appropriate analogous niche is that of the living wolves who hunt and live in packs and cover extraordinarily broad ranges in their hunt (Peters & Mech, 1975). In the differences in sensory and motor capacities between advanced land carnivores, such as wolves, and advanced social primates, such as baboons and African apes, we may find the clue to the evolution of speech and language.

Unlike the higher primates, wolves have a highly evolved olfactory system and a system for marking a trail and range. Their olfactory systems enable them to follow a trail and note the limits of the range; the marking system (through urine and scent glands) may enable them to define the trail and the range, both for their individual use and for the use of other members of their group and potential competitors. Wolves also produce characteristic (though stereotyped) calls useful for communication, but are relatively limited in their capacity to manipulate objects in their environment. They are visually inadequate compared to primates, with visual systems only marginally adapted for daylight vision and most effective in twilight.

Higher primates are almost pathetically lacking in an olfactory apparatus, and humans are among the poorest of the higher primates in this regard. It is difficult for us to imagine the reality that a wolf or almost any other land mammal perceives because we are so "blind" with respect to the olfactory world that must be so rich for other animals. On the other hand, primates (including man) are the most visual of mammals, unusually well adapted for daylight vision and reasonably adapted for nocturnal vision. With respect to vocalization, most higher primates are at least as competent as wolves with an extensive repertoire of generally stereotyped calls used to signal a variety of emotional states. In auditory capacities primates and wolves are comparable, both being about as sensitive as it is possible for any animal to be to very weak sounds in the middle-frequency range.

The essential feature in this hypothesis is that the early hominids must be imagined as social predators. They would thus have been widely dispersed, living in small groups that covered enormous ranges. They had to do this without the typical mammalian predator's armament of olfactory sensitivity and scent-making capacities. I see the early use of language as a system for coping with an extended range, marking it vocally by identifying (naming) some features in it and vocalizing and hearing the vocalization. This could produce an internalized map of the range, and by the use of vocalization the early hominids could identify and communicate their presence at distant parts of the range. The strong visual sense could contribute to this identified reality. Such improved capacity for imagery would enable the members of a group to reidentify a range or a trail from the restated calls or names, even if one assumes no improved capacity for storage, or memory, compared to that of other progressive mammals.

The resulting picture is of wide-ranging predators using linguistic forms to map their range and territory. Early language contributed to the capacity for imagery rather than for communication.

There is an interesting twist to this analysis. If we have a species in which imagery has auditory and vocal as well as visual and other sensory components, and if heard and produced and imagined sound is a central part of the imagery, a novel social behavior could evolve. By appropriate vocalization one animal in a group could evoke images of geographical maps or other events in other animals in the group. It is in such shared imagery, rather than communication in the usual sense, that I would identify the beginning of speech and language. Since a perceptual domain is involved, we are not surprised to find that the details of the speech and language, unlike communication in other mammals, are strongly dependent on the early experiences of the members of the group in their exposure to the sensorimotor (especially speech and language) world of their group. The twist in the analysis is in our recognition that sensory activity, like language, is to a significant extent learned, whereas nonhuman communication usually involves major innate behavior adaptations.

To present the results of this evolutionary point of view in another way, let us consider how language is used in our own lives. We recognize that the "imperative" in communication, in which we elicit actions from others—that is, direct their actions—can be accomplished with a limited repertoire of conventional signs: pointing, shaking one's head or hand, nonverbal shouts or hisses, and so forth. We need and use language to tell stories and produce complex images in our readers and listeners rather than to direct their actions. There are few experiences more compelling than those that we enter vicariously through the language of the storyteller whose stories may be in the form of words on a printed page. We can live the lives of the characters in a well-executed realistic novel so completely that everything else may fade from consciousness. This is the true function of language, I submit, and it demonstrates the role of language as an element in our capacity to imagine, which I equate with our capacity to experience a real world. The world of imagination and the world of immediate experience are comparable worlds from this point of view, although it is obviously also necessary to be able to encode the fact that events in imagination and events in experience are different. We normally do this automatically, of course, and have no difficulty in distinguishing image from reality, though, as they do in dreams, the two can merge.

From the evolution of the brain we have progressed without difficulty to the evolution of mind. The latter should be thought of as a natural development of a certain aspect of the brain's work: the creation of a real world to explain the mass of incoming and outgoing information processed by the brain. The information, which is in the form of neural electrochemical messages, is so vast that without clumping of some kind it could not be handled (Simon, 1974). The clumping, I suggested, was by encoding the information as objects (including the self) acting in space and time, and the actions could be in the imagination as well as in the world of immediate experience.

The peculiarly human relevance of this analysis is for our understanding of the meaning of intelligence as a biological phenomenon. This point of view would consider biological intelligence as a measure of the quality of the real worlds created by the nervous systems of different species. Variations might occur within a species, but they would be minor variations on the major theme in evolution.

The human real world is one massively affected by the evolution of language and linguistic forms. it may, thus, not be entirely accidental that in the creation of tests of human intelligence the testers have produced instruments that measure verbal capacities to the extent that they do, and find it so difficult to construct nonverbal tests that do not correlate strongly with simple measures of verbal ability. A nonverbal test of intelligence may be a contradiction in terms, in the deep sense, because even if words are avoided in the test, the language and language-related functions of the human brain are inevitably dominant in most human performance.*

*   *   *

BAILLARGER, J. De l'étendue de la surface du cerveau et de ses rapports avec le développement de l'intelligence. *Annales Médico-Psychologiques.* 2 série, 1853, *5*, 1-9.

BLAKEMORE, C. Developmental factors in the formation of feature extracting neurons. In F. O. Schmitt & F. G. Warden (Eds.), *The neurosciences: Third study program.* Cambridge: MIT Press, 1974.

*These concluding sentences emphasize the unity of mind. They are not entirely consistent with the conclusions presented in other chapters that describe the specializations of the two cerebral hemispheres for different kinds of cognitive information processing. At issue is whether to emphasize the integrative or the specialized functions of the brain. I emphasize the integrative functions. In an evolutionary context, the various specialized functions of the human brain associated with **hemispheric lateralization** and asymmetry seem to be uniquely human adaptations. I associate them with the evolution of the capacity for imagery that is a languagelike, cognitive contribution to the meaning of an image, whether the contribution arises from verbal-grammatical analysis or spatial-configurational analysis. Some of the experimental evidence for the integrative functions in normal human behavior has been summarized by Broadbent (1974) who pointed out that "the two hemispheres must be seen . . . as performing different parts of an integrated performance, rather than completely separate and parallel functions" (p. 31).

BROADBENT, D. E. Division of function and integration of behavior. In F. O. Schmitt and F. G. Warden (Eds.), *The neurosciences: Third study program*. Cambridge: MIT Press, 1974.

BUTCHER, H. J. *Human intelligence*. London: Methuen, 1968.

DARWIN, C. *The descent of man and selection in relation to sex*. London: Murray, 1871. Reprinted with *The origin of species*. New York: Modern Library, 1936.

DOBZHANSKY, T. *Genetics of the evolutionary process*. New York: Columbia University Press, 1970.

FALCONER, D. S. Genetic consequences of selection pressure. In J. E. Meade & A. S. Parkes (Eds.), *Genetic and environmental factors in human ability*. Edinburgh: Oliver and Boyd, 1966.

FISHER, R. A. *The genetical theory of natural selection*. Oxford: Clarendon Press, 1930.

GRABINER, J. V., & MILLER, P. D. Effects of the Scopes trial. *Science*, 1974, *185*, 832-837.

HINDE, R. A. (Ed.). *Bird vocalization: Essays presented to W. H. Thorpe*. New York: Cambridge University Press, 1969.

HODOS, W. Evolutionary interpretation of neural and behavioral studies of living vertebrates. In F. O. Schmitt (Ed.), *The neurosciences: Second study program*. New York: Rockefeller University Press, 1970.

HOLLOWAY, R. L. The casts of fossil hominid brains. *Scientific American*, 1974, *231*(1), 106-115.

HUXLEY, T. H. *Man's place in nature*. London: Williams and Norgate, 1863.

JERISON, H. J. *Evolution of the brain and intelligence*. New York: Academic Press, 1973.

JERISON, H. J. Fossil evidence of the evolution of the hominid brain. *Annual Review of Anthropology*, 1975, *4*, 27-58.

JERISON, H. J. Paleoneurology and the evolution of mind. *Scientific American*, 1976, *234*(1), 90-101. (a)

JERISON, H. J. Discussion paper: The paleoneurology of language. *Annals of the New York Academy of Sciences*, 1976, *280*, 370-382. (b)

JERISON, H. J. The theory of encephalization. *Annals of the New York Academy of Sciences,* 1977, *299,* 146-160.

KUHN, T. C. *The structure of scientific revolutions* (2nd ed.). Chicago: University of Chicago Press, 1970.

LASHLEY, K. S. Persistent problems in the evolution of mind. *Quarterly Review of Biology,* 1949, *24,* 28-42.

LEGROS CLARK, W. E. Deformation patterns in the cerebral cortex. In W. E. LeGros Clark & P. B. Medawar (Eds.), *Essays on growth and form presented to D'Arcy Wentworth Thompson.* London and New York: Oxford University Press, 1945.

LEMAY, M., & CULEBRAS, A. Human brain: Morphologic differences in the hemispheres demonstrable by carotid arteriography. *New England Journal of Medicine,* 1972, *287,* 268-270.

LEWONTIN, R. C. *The genetic basis of evolutionary change.* New York: Columbia University Press, 1974.

McCLEARN, G. E., & DeFRIES, J. C. *Introduction to behavior genetics.* San Francisco: Freeman, 1973.

METTLER, F. A. Culture and the structural evolution of the neural system. James Arthur Lecture, New York, American Museum of Natural History, 1956.

OSTROM, J. H. *Archaeopteryx* and the origin of flight. *Quarterly Review of Biology,* 1974, *49,* 27-47.

PETERS, R. P. & MECH, L. D. Scent-marking in wolves. *American Scientist,* 1975, *63,* 628-637.

POLYAK, S. *The vertebrate visual system.* (H. Kluver, Ed.) Chicago: University of Chicago Press, 1957.

POPPER, K. *Objective knowledge.* London: Oxford University Press, 1972.

RADINSKY, L. Evolution of the canid brain. *Brain, Behavior, and Evolution,* 1973, *7,* 169-202.

SHERRINGTON, C. S. *Man on his nature* (2nd ed.). New Haven: Yale University Press, 1950.

SIMON, H. A. How big is a chunk? *Science,* 1974, *183,* 482-488.

SIMPSON, G. G. *The major features of evolution.* New York: Columbia University Press, 1953.

SIMPSON, G. G. *This view of life.* New York: Harcourt, 1964.

SIMPSON, G. G. Uniformitarianism. An inquiry into principle, theory, and method in geohistory and biohistory. In M.K. Hecht & W. C. Steere (Eds.), *Essays in evolution and genetics in honor of Theodosius Dobzhansky.* Amsterdam: North Holland Publishing Co. 1970.

TEUBER, H. L. Why two brains? In F. O. Schmitt & F. G. Worden (Eds.), *The neurosciences: Third study program.* Cambridge: MIT Press, 1974.

THORPE, W. J. *Learning and instinct in animals.* London: Metheun, 1956.

TOBIAS, P. V. Brain-size, grey matter, and race—fact or fiction? *American Journal of Physical Anthropology,* 1970, *32,* 3-26.

TOBIAS, P.V. *The brain in hominid evolution.* New York: Columbia University Press, 1971.

VON BONIN, G. *The evolution of the human brain.* Chicago: University of Chicago Press, 1963.

VON UEXKÜLL, J. Streifzüge durch die Umwelten von Tieren und Menschen. In C. H. Schiller (Ed. and Trans.), *Instinctive behavior: The development of a modern concept.* New York: International Universities Press, 1957. (Originally published 1934.)

3

Activation and Attention in the Human Brain

by Jackson Beatty

The cortex is not isolated from the rest of the brain. Before discussing the hemispheric processes of the brain in Chapters 4, 5, and 6, we should look at some of the close relationships which exist between the cortex and the brainstem. In the following chapter, Dr. Jackson Beatty of the UCLA Department of Psychology and Brain Research Institute, explains two current approaches to the study of how the brainstem participates with the cortex in the processing of information. The first approach measures momentary changes in attention as they occur in perception, short-term memory, and problem solving. These momentary changes of attention are measured by changes in the diameter of the pupils of the eyes. In the second approach, longer-lasting changes in attention, called sustained attention, are studied with brain-wave recordings obtained during lengthy monotonous tasks, such as long-distance freeway driving. Dr. Beatty reports interesting findings about how changes come about in patterns of brain activity reflecting the involvement of the brainstem and the cortex according to the nature of the problems confronted by the brain. By understanding something about the physical basis of attention, the educator may be able to adapt instructional procedures to minimize attentional problems in education.

Everyone knows what attention is. It is the taking possession by the mind, in clear and vivid form of one out of what seem several simultaneously possible objects or trains of thought. Focalization, concentration, of consciousness are of its essence. It implies withdrawal from some things in order to deal effectively with others. . . . Fatigue, monotonous mechanical occupations that end by being automatically carried on, tend to produce (a state of nonattention) in men. It is not sleep; and yet when aroused from such a state, a person will often hardly be able to say what he has been thinking about. . . . (William James, 1890, pp. 403–405).

At least three separate meanings for the term *attention* may be found in these words of William James, the celebrated American psychologist who wrote his *Principles of Psychology* at the end of the nineteenth century. James's *attention* is at once a *selective* process, in which some things are perceived and others are not; an *intensive* process, in which more or less effort or concentration is employed; and a *sustaining* process, which acts to maintain the general capacity of the organism to process information during monotonous, repetitive tasks in unstimulating environments. These three meanings in fact refer to different aspects of attention, which, although related to each other and interdependent, are nonetheless at least partially distinct and separable.

Unfortunately, the problem of attention in its various aspects faded from American psychology in the early years of this century and remained virtually unstudied until the 1950s. The reasons for this are several, but they primarily reflect the widespread belief in those years that behavior could be understood as a set of more or less fixed relations between stimulus events and responses, with little regard for active intervening processes. The reemergence of attention as a compelling problem for psychology developed, in large part, in response to advances made in the areas of neurophysiology, neuroanatomy, neuropsychology, and physiological psychology that began to reveal the complexity of brain processes that mediate behavior. In particular, the physiological and behavioral work that followed Moruzzi and Magoun's (1949) discovery of the reticular system's role in regulating brain **activation** played an important role in reawakening scientific interest in the problem of attention. Activation is a physiological concept that refers to brain mechanisms that control behavioral arousal. Subsequent work has led to a new conception of the relations between the cortex, which contains the circuitry directly responsible for complex information processing, and the brainstem, which lies beneath it. Higher cortical information-processing functions began to be seen as dependent upon the integrative, activating processes of the brainstem core. This view suggested that the behavioral phenomena of attention in its various aspects might be related to the physiological processes of activation (Lindsley, 1960).

In the present chapter, two experimental approaches to the study of attention that we have employed in our laboratories are presented. Both are concerned with the relations between measures of brain activation and behavioral attention. The first, which investigates peripheral signs of momentary changes in activation that occur during **cognitive processing**, attempts to discover the empirical relations between activation and *intensive* attention. The second explores the relationship between longer-lasting changes in cortical activation as they are related to *sustained* attention and performance in prolonged monotonous vigilance tasks. These two lines of experimental research are illustrative of current work on the neuropsychology of attention in man.

The reader who is interested in the problem of attention is referred to a number of excellent reviews which have been published in recent years. The problem of selective attention has been extensively treated with both behavioral and physiological methods. This work is summarized in reviews by Broadbent (1970), Egeth (1967), Kahneman (1973), Moray (1969a, 1969b),

Swets and Kristofferson (1970), and Treisman (1969). The question of intensive attention has been less fully explored, but the books by Kahneman (1973) and Norman (1976) review much of what is now known in this area. Several volumes have also been published that treat sustained attention in considerable detail (Davies & Tune, 1969; Mackworth, 1969, 1970; Mostofsky, 1970; Stroh, 1971).

Measuring Activation

Several different methods may be employed to measure nervous system activation, each having its own particular strengths and weaknesses. Measuring cortical brain rhythms is one obvious choice, since these waves originate in the cortex itself. Further, there are well-known relations between EEG (electroencephalogram) patterns and activation; thus the desynchronization of ongoing brain rhythms as evidenced in the EEG may be taken as an indication of cortical activation with a fair amount of certainty (Lindsley, 1960). However, with conventional analysis procedures, a considerable period of EEG activity must be analyzed to yield a stable estimate of cortical **synchrony** or **desynchrony** (Kellaway & Petersen, 1973). For this reason, EEG measures of synchrony and desynchrony are more useful as indicators of activation over long periods of time, as in the study of sustained attention, than as indicators of momentary activation shifts required in the study of intensive attention.

Another class of EEG analysis procedures involves measuring small electrical events occurring in cortex immediately following the presentation of brief stimuli. These *event-related cortical potentials,* as they are called, have been studied in a wide variety of information-processing situations, and the results of such experiments have been extensively reviewed elsewhere (Karlin,

1970; McCallum & Knott, 1973; Picton & Hillyard, 1974; Posner, 1975; Tecce, 1970, 1972). Event-related cortical potentials have proven useful in the analysis of both intensive and sustained attention.

A third procedure for studying the rapid shifts in nervous system activation in cognitive processing is based upon the fact that changes in nervous system activation are present not only in the activity of the cortex, but also appear in the peripheral portions of the nervous system, particularly in the autonomic nervous system. Of the various peripheral indicators of autonomic activation, the movements of the pupil of the eye are perhaps best suited for investigating the relationships between activation and thought (Kahneman, Tursky, Shapiro, & Crider, 1969; Loewenfeld, 1958).

As early as 1920, Lowenstein recognized that the pupil of the eye dilates (widens) during cognitive activity (Goldwater, 1972). These dilations may be observed under conditions of constant illumination and are quite independent of the well-known light reflex, which constricts the pupil as illumination increases. Pupillary movements are produced by changes in the relative activation of two muscle groups in the iris. One set of iris musculature, the *dilator pupillae*, are radially oriented smooth muscle fibers that are innervated by fibers from the sympathetic branch of the autonomic nervous system. Sympathetic activation, therefore, acts to dilate the pupils. Functionally and structurally opposed to the dilator pupillae are the parasympathetically innervated muscles called the *sphincter pupillae*, which constrict the pupil as they contract. Thus momentary pupillary diameter reflects the activation of both sympathetic and parasympathetic musculature. In terms of gross autonomic function, pupillary dilation may be interpreted as a sign of autonomic activation. However, it is only in the last few decades that the systematic nature of the relations between autonomic activation and cognitive processing have become apparent (Goldwater, 1972; Janisse, 1974). Pupillometric analysis provides a method by which to undertake the study of activation and the higher cognitive processes of the human brain, since the pupillary peripheral signs of autonomic activation are readily measurable in man.

Intensive Attention, Processing Load, and Task-induced Changes in Activation

The *activation theory of intensive attention* proposes that cognitive processes require specifiable amounts of intensive attention or "mental effort" for their execution and that the momentary level of effort involved is reflected in momentary increases in brain activation, which may be measured by appropriate physiological techniques (Kahneman, 1973). The theory predicts that the activation increases should be larger for more difficult processing functions and should be related in a systematic fashion to the momentary level of effort required to perform those functions. The idea is that cognitive functions can be characterized by their information-processing load — the demands for capacity that they impose upon the organism — and that this processing load can be measured by the momentary level of task-induced activation (Kahneman & Beatty, 1966). We proposed a simple analogy (Kahneman & Beatty, 1967) to clarify this idea: In a home filled with a variety of electrical appliances, the total demand for electrical power rises and falls as the appliances are switched on and off. The momentary level of demand for power could be measured using the appropriate instrument attached to the electrical line outside the house. Information-processing load was conceived as analogous to the total demand for power required to perform a particular set of information-processing functions at a particular moment in time. Notice that this concept depends not so much upon what stimuli are presented to the organism, but upon the internal processes that the organism uses to handle environmental information.

Autonomic activation may, under appropriately specified circumstances, reflect cortical demands for momentary activation by the brainstem to permit cortical processing of complex information. For this reason, the study of pupillary movements during cognitive processing may reflect momentary changes in brain activation that are directly related to task-induced changes in cognitive capacity. A variety of lines of experimental evidence support this hypothesis.

PERCEPTUAL DETECTION

Even the apparently simple processes of sensory perception place processing demands upon the human brain that can be measured by changes in the diameter of the pupil. For example, Hakerem and Sutton (1966) measured pupillary responses to light flashes at intensities near the limits of visual perception. These visual stimuli were too weak to elicit the well-known pupillary constriction to light and were in fact only barely perceptible, being reported as seen on only 50 percent of the **trials**. There was no pupillary dilation following visual stimuli that were not detected by the viewer, nor did dilations appear if the viewer was not asked to attempt to discriminate the weak flashes. But if a discrimination (flash present or absent) was required and a flash was detected, a clear pupillary dilation appeared. Hakerem and Sutton believed this reflected the cortical demands for activation necessary to process the detected stimulus.

We have completed a similar set of experiments on the perception of weak acoustic signals and have found very similar results (Beatty, 1975). In one of these studies listeners attempted to detect a weak tone against a background of acoustic noise — a tone which was in fact present on only one-half of all trials. When the exact time that the signal might appear was uncertain, no dilations were observed in the absence of a signal or in the presence of an undetected signal. As in Hakerem and Sutton's experiment, the pupillary dilation indicating cortical activation occurred only when a presented signal was actually detected by the listener. These dilations occur with great reliability, indicating that the activation changes that they reflect are a constant accompaniment of perceptual processing. In fact, it was possible to predict the listener's judgment from the pupillary data alone with between 66 and 92 percent accuracy. Regular changes in nervous system activation appear to accompany even the simplest acts of sensory registration and decision.

PERCEPTUAL DISCRIMINATION

More difficult perceptual discriminations place greater demands upon the human brain, demands reflected in increased levels of task-induced activation. For example, in a tone-discrimination task in which the listener must decide whether the second of two tones is higher in pitch than the first, the degree of dilation following the presentation of the comparison tone varies directly as a function of task difficulty (Kahneman & Beatty, 1967). The standard tone in that experiment was always a 850-Hz (Hz = cycles per second) sine wave; the comparison tones ranged from 820 to 880 Hz in 6 Hz steps. Maximal dilations were observed following comparison tones of 850 Hz (an impossible discrimination). The greater the difference in frequency between standard and comparison, the easier was the discrimination (as measured by the percentage of errors) and the smaller was the dilation observed in the decision interval following the presentation of the comparison tone.

SHORT-TERM MEMORY

Perhaps the most striking data on the relations between activation and cognitive processing comes from the study of serial short-term memory. In these experiments, subjects are presented with strings of items which they are to recall in strict serial order after a few seconds' delay. Retaining a new telephone number while dialing is one example of a serial short-term memory task that is common in everyday life. Such tasks are **resource-limited** (Norman & Bobrow, 1975), in that the number of items that might be held in short-term memory for immediate recall reflects limits in the subject's capacity to process information.

In the first experiment **pupillometrically** measuring activation in serial recall (Kahneman & Beatty, 1966) five undergraduate students listened to strings of between 3 and 7 digits (the approximate limit of immediate memory for digit strings) presented at the rate of 1 per second. After a 2-second pause, they repeated back each string at the same rate. Figure 3.1 presents these data. Since the strings were of different length, trial duration also varied between conditions. Therefore, the data are aligned at the pause, with the beginning of presentation and the termination of response indicated on each curve by slash markers.

Several points emerge from these data. First, the pupil dilates as each digit is presented, reaching a maximal dilation after all digits are presented. Second, as each item in the string is reported by the listener — and the momentary load on immediate memory decreases — the pupil constricts, returning to its initial level as the last digit is reported. Third, the amount of dilation at the pause between digit input and output is a **monotonic function** of the number of items held in immediate memory. These data strongly suggest that pupillary dilation varies directly with momentary cognitive load.

If these pupillometric changes reflect processing load in the

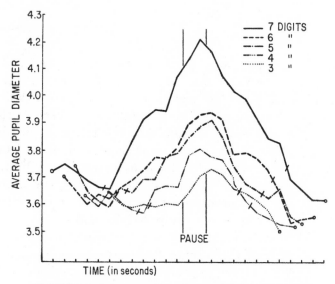

FIGURE 3.1. Average pupillary diameter in millimeters during presentation and recall of strings of 3, 4, 5, 6, or 7 digits. Slash marks on the left of the figure indicate the start of digit presentation and those on the right indicate the end of the subject's report. These curves are of different lengths, since digits were presented and reported at a constant rate of 1 per second. For this reason, the curves from all conditions are centered about the 2-second pause between stimulus presentation and subject report. (From Kahneman & Beatty in *Science,* 1966, *154* (3756), 1583–1585, with permission of the publisher.)

serial memory task, then the slope of the function should increase when more difficult items are used in the test. This would appear as a larger dilation for each item at input and a greater constriction for each item at output. A second portion of the experiment compared both performance and activation functions for strings of 4 digits, 4 words, and a transformation of 4 digits (adding 1 to each of the previously presented digits in report).* These latter two tasks are more difficult than the simple digit task: In preexperimental testing of these subjects mean (average) digit span

*For example, in the transformation task, if the listener heard "5, 8, 3, 7," he should say "6, 9, 4, 8."

was 7.8 items, mean word span was 5.7 items, and mean transformation span was 4.5 items. Thus, these three tests should differ in processing load, with larger dilations occurring for each item of the more difficult materials. Figure 3.2 presents the pupillometric data for this portion of the experiment. Both the slope and the maximal dilation on each of the three tests reflect the level of processing load associated with the item difficulty. Larger dilations are present for the storage of items requiring greater processing capacity.

Similar activation patterns appear when material is retrieved from permanent memory and organized in immediate memory for serial report. In one experiment (Beatty & Kahneman, 1966), for example, subjects were required to recall a familiar telephone number when presented with a one-word

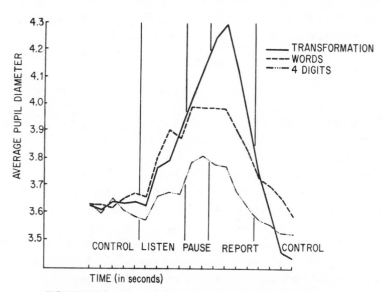

FIGURE 3.2. Average pupillary diameter in millimeters during presentation, pause, and report of 4 digits, 4 words, and the transformation of a string of 4 digits by adding 1 to each digit heard before report. (From Kahneman & Beatty in *Science,* 1966, *154* (3756), 1583–1585, with permission of the publisher.)

name associated with that number, such as *home* or *office*, and to report that number at a 1-digit per second rate. In this situation the pupil immediately dilated following the memory cue as the telephone number was retrieved and prepared for report. The magnitude of this dilation was larger than that seen in the same subjects when presented with a string of 7 unfamiliar digits for serial recall. The difference may be related to the load imposed in retrieving information from permanent memory. During report, pupillary diameter decreased with each digit spoken, returning to baseline diameter as the last digit of the telephone number was reported (see Figure 3.3).

Thus in serial memory tasks processing load is not stationary or fixed, but varies from second to second as the number of items that must be held in immediate memory increases and decreases. The pattern of pupillary dilation accurately reflects these shifting demands. Further, when item difficulty is increased, the magnitude of the activation changes also increases.

PROBLEM SOLVING

In problem solving, as in perceptual and memory tasks, **phasic** activation changes may be measured pupillometrically that appear to be related to fundamental aspects of task-related information processing. For example, Hess and Polt (1964) obtained pupillary measurements as subjects mentally solved simple multiplication problems. After presentation of each problem, pupillary diameter slowly increased, reaching maximal dilation immediately before solution. Following solution and report, the pupil rapidly returned to its initial diameter. The extent of dilation at solution was a function of presumed problem difficulty or processing load: An average dilation of 10.8 percent was reported for the simplest problem (7 × 8) as compared with 21.6 percent for the most difficult (16 × 23). Dilations to problems of intermediate difficulty fell between these two extremes.

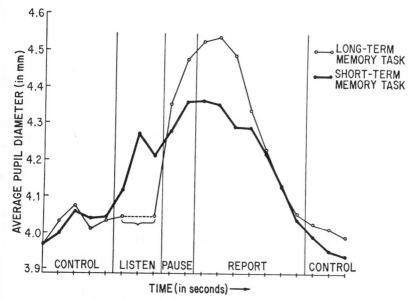

FIGURE 3.3 Average pupillary diameter during presentation and report of 7-digit telephone numbers from long-term and short-term or immediate memory. Stimulus presentation required 2 seconds longer in the short-term memory condition, in which the entire string of digits was read to the subject, than in the long-term memory condition, in which a single word such as *home* or *office* was used to identify the digit string for report. For this reason, the long-term memory function is broken above the trace, with both points representing the same pupillary measurement. (From Beatty & Kahneman in *Psychonomic Science,* 1966, *5* (10), 371–372, with permission of the publisher.)

Payne, Parry, and Harasymiw (1968) report a similar relationship between pupillary dilation and difficulty in mental multiplication problems. Four levels of problem difficulty were employed, in which a single-digit multiplier was used with a 1- to 4-digit multiplicand. As in the Hess and Polt experiment, a pupillary dilation appeared in the interval between problem presentation and report of solution, the degree of dilation being a monotonic function of problem difficulty. The largest difference in dilation appeared between difficulty levels 1 and 2.

Rather small increases in mean dilation were observed between levels 2, 3, and 4, although total processing time increased in the expected manner. Pupil data suggest that rather different internal processes may be operating in problems with single-digit as compared with multiple-digit multiplicands. Specifically, problems with multiple-digit multiplicands require that intermediate results be stored in memory as each successive digit of the multiplicand is being processed, with processing time being a function of the number of such steps necessary to complete the problem.

The conclusion from all of this is that very rapid, phasic changes in activation accompany cognitive processing. The amount of the activation appears to be directly related to the momentary level of cognitive load imposed by the information-processing task. The reliability of these activation changes suggests that they are intimately involved in complex information-processing functions. However, there are no data available at present to indicate clearly the details of the relation between phasic activation changes and cortical processing; indeed, without a reasonable understanding of the cortical mechanisms involved in specific information-processing functions it is virtually impossible to propose in concrete form the role that activation might play in facilitating them. However, the knowledge that complex cortical functions appear to be activation-dependent might prove a clue for future work on the nature of cortical mechanisms mediating complex information processing in man.

Sustained Attention

Research on sustained attention has focused upon watchkeeping tasks, in which people are required to monitor a monotonous display for long periods of time in search of infrequent signals.

Industrial inspection is one everyday example of a situation requiring sustained attention. Radar monitoring at sea and long-distance freeway driving are others. In such tasks, performance usually deteriorates as a function of time spent continuously working. These tasks have been termed "vigilance" tasks. The assumption underlying much research on sustained attention is that performance is limited by a decline of nervous system "vigilance" (a British term that is roughly equivalent to the American "activation"). The activation hypothesis predicts that performance should deteriorate as the level of nervous system activation declines over time in the task. There is a reasonable body of evidence that supports the idea that the failure of sustained attention under such conditions is the result of a steady decline in nervous system activation. Most of this evidence comes from correlational experiments, in which both performance and brain activation are measured concurrently as a person performs a vigilance-type task for prolonged periods.

Of the various physiological measurements of activation, the most interesting for our purposes is the electroencephalogram or EEG. The EEG (see Chapter 1) is a recording of brain activity made from electrodes placed upon the scalp. For this reason, the EEG cannot reflect the individual patterns of firing of single cortical cells, or even small groups of such cells. The electrical signals recordable from the human scalp reflect simultaneously occurring electrical events in very large numbers of neurons located between the recording electrodes. (In addition, other electrical signs of bodily processes such as skeletal muscle activity or contraction of the heart muscles may appear in the EEG tracing, but with careful recording techniques, these sources of electrical activity can largely be removed from the EEG.) EEG recordings have proven to be very useful as indicators of the general state of cortical activation, in discerning the various states of sleep, and in indexing the relative level of alertness in the waking brain (Rechtschaffen & Kales, 1968; Lindsley, 1960).

For example, in the awake and alerted human brain, the

EEG picture is characterized by a pattern of low-voltage fast activity, indicating desynchrony of the cortical neurons that generate the EEG (see Fig. 1.9). Such a pattern often alternates with periods of synchronous higher voltage activity at about 10 Hz, the alpha rhythm of the human brain. As alertness declines, however, desynchrony occurs less frequently and the pattern of alpha activity becomes less well organized. Periods of lower-amplitude, poorly organized activity in the theta frequencies (4 to 8 Hz) may then begin to appear.

Groll (1966) measured various indicators of nervous system activation, including EEG, as volunteers performed a 90-minute sequential brightness discrimination task while laying supine, a condition that is likely to produce decreasing activation over time. Groll reported that both the percentage of correct detections and the average EEG frequency decreased as the monitoring task progressed. This is in keeping with the idea that sustained attention depends upon the maintenance of an appropriate level of activation in the brain. Further, Groll reported differences in the EEG pattern in the period immediately preceding signals that were correctly detected and signals that were missed. The mean EEG frequency preceding detections tended to be in the alpha range, whereas theta activity appeared in the EEG before misses. This suggests that the momentary state of cortical activation is related to the efficiency with which the brain can process environmental information.

Similar findings had previously been reported by Williams (Williams, Granda, Jones, Lubin, & Armington, 1962) for sleep-deprived persons exposed to conditions of monotonous monitoring requiring sustained attention, although the relation between theta activity in the posterior cortex and performance was not apparent under rested conditions. This discrepancy may result from the fact that Williams used visual methods of EEG scoring, which are less sensitive and less accurate than the more modern computer-aided techniques of EEG classification. However, not all investigators have found this theoretically predictable relation between increases in posterior theta activity and performance decrement. Daniel (1967), in an experiment that remains anomolous and contradictory, found less theta activity preceding missed signals than correctly detected ones.

One difficulty with all of these experiments is that they rely upon correlations between brain activity and behavior that unfold during prolonged periods of monotonous activity. The validity of the relation between brain activation and vigilance performance would be more firmly established if one could independently regulate the level of alertness in the observer while performing a vigilance-type task. One possible experimental approach to this question is to train people using **operant** or **biofeedback** techniques to control brain activation by regulating the posterior theta rhythm, which we have seen is a useful electroencephalographic indicator of the state of cortical arousal. The activation theory of sustained attention predicts that EEG regulation should maintain attention and prevent the vigilance decrement in subjects trained to suppress posterior theta frequency activity, whereas regulation should degrade performance and further impair performance in subjects previously trained to increase theta activity.

In collaboration with James O'Hanlon we undertook an experiment using operant regulation of the EEG in an attempt to gain a better understanding of the physiological basis of sustained attention (Beatty, Greenberg, Deibler, & O'Hanlon, 1974). The plan of the experiment was simple: First, using operant biofeedback methods, some subjects were trained to suppress posterior theta activity and others were trained to increase it. Then all subjects were tested twice in a vigilance-type task, once while using feedback to regulate their EEGs as they had previously been trained and once with the EEG unregulated. Nineteen paid student volunteers were trained to regulate the proportion of theta frequency activity in the posterior EEG using standard biofeedback and operant procedures (see Beatty & Legewie, 1977, or Schwartz & Beatty, 1977, for fuller reviews of the operant modification of physiological events). Of these, twelve were trained to suppress and seven to increase posterior theta activity. All had achieved control within two one-hour practice sessions. These students were also familiarized with a simulated radar-observation task, which required monitoring a visual display for a period of 2 hours to detect infrequently occurring weak radarlike signals.

After this pretraining, each volunteer was tested in two monitoring sessions, one with and one without the feedback signal necessary to regulate the EEG. The results of this experiment were exactly as predicted by the activation theory of sustained attention (see Figure 3.4). In the absence of feedback, both groups showed a decreasing level of performance over the 2-hour period of the watch. When tested with feedback, however, the two groups behaved very differently. No vigilance decrement or impairment of performance occurred during the task for subjects trained to suppress EEG theta, whereas an increased vigilance decrement appeared for those subjects trained to increase theta activity. In other words, when operant procedures are employed as an independent means of regulating the level of cortical arousal, as indexed by the proportion of theta-frequency activity in the posterior EEG, behavioral performance in a sustained attention or vigilance task is systematically affected. Operantly maintained cortical activation or alertness abolishes the vigilance decrement, whereas operantly induced cortical deactivation acts to further degrade performance in a task requiring sustained attention. These findings, together with the previously observed correlation between decline in performance as a function of time on the task and a decline in physiological indicators of cortical activation, lend substantial support to the link proposed between sustained attention and the **tonic level** of nervous system activation.

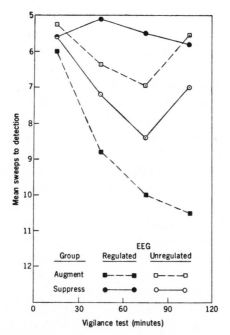

FIGURE 3.4. Mean time required to detect a target (indicated as the number of 6-second sweeps of the radar display required before detection) as a function of time in the vigilance test for the theta-augment and the theta-suppress groups with EEG regulated and unregulated. Notice that the ordinate (vertical) scale is inverted. Theta suppression appears to improve performance and theta augmentation to degrade performance with respect to the EEG-unregulated conditions. (From Beatty, Greenberg, Deibler, & O'Hanlon in *Science,* 1974, *183,* 871–873, with permission of the publisher.)

Some Difficulties

The activation theories of intensive and sustained attention have received considerable empirical support, as the experimental evidence discussed above would indicate, but they are not without some problems. First, although both intensive and sustained attention are closely related to brain activation processes, the interrelations between phasic activation and **tonic** activation are far from clear. Tonic and phasic activation processes appear to operate with some degree of independence. For example, over a short series of auditory discrimination trials, a tonic measure of activation may decline markedly, whereas a phasic measure reflecting task-induced activation changes occurring on each trial may remain constant from beginning to end (Kahneman & Beatty, 1967). These two kinds of processes are clearly complex, and a similar level of complexity is required for any general theory of brain activation treating both kinds of data.

Second, the mechanism by which brainstem activation processes affect the efficiency of cortical information processing remains puzzling. At the cortical level, activation means something other than simple excitation; the average rate of firing in most cortical neurons does not increase markedly during activation. Rather, it is the patterning of firing that appears to be changed. In visual cortex, for example, during activation, cells become more responsive to sensory stimulation without grossly changing their firing rates (Evarts, 1963). The way in which this reorganization is accomplished is presently unknown.

Third, the various signs taken as indicators of nervous system activation are not always in perfect agreement. Activation therefore cannot be a unitary process and care must be exercised to specify exactly what measures of nervous system activity are taken as indicators of activation in any particular instance.

Yet it is clear that brain activation mechanisms and behavioral attention processes are intimately related. The task is to explore more deeply and to clarify more exactly the nature of these relationships.

*   *   *

BEATTY, J. Prediction of detection of weak acoustic signals from patterns of pupillary activity preceding behavioral response. UCLA Technical Report, May 27, 1975.

BEATTY, J.; GREENBERG, A.; DEIBLER, W. P.; & O'HANLON, J. F. Operant control of occipital theta rhythm affects performance in a radar monitoring task. *Science*, 1974, *183*, 871-873.

BEATTY, J., & KAHNEMAN, D. Pupillary changes in two memory tasks. *Psychonomic Science*, 1966, *5*, 371-372.

BEATTY, J., & LEGEWIE, H. *Biofeedback and behavior*. New York: Plenum, 1977.

BROADBENT, D. E. Stimulus set and response set: Two kinds of selective attention. In D. I. Mostofsky (Ed.), *Attention: Contemporary theory and analysis*. New York: Appleton-Century-Crofts, 1970.

DANIEL, R. S. Alpha and theta EEG in vigilance. *Perceptual and Motor Skills*, 1967, *25*, 697-703.

DAVIES, D. R., & TUNE, G. S. *Human vigilance performance*. New York: American Elsevier, 1969.

EGETH, H. Selective attention. *Psychological Bulletin*, 1967, *67*, 41-57.

EVARTS, E. V. Photically evoked responses in visual cortex units during sleep and waking. *Journal of Neurophysiology*, 1963, *26*, 229-248.

GOLDWATER, B. C. Psychological significance of pupillary movements. *Psychological Bulletin*, 1972, *77*, 340-355.

GROLL, E. Central nervous system and peripheral activation variables during vigilance performance. (In German, English summary). *Zeitschrift für Experimentelle und Angewandte Psychologie*, 1966, *13*, 248-264.

HAKEREM, G., & SUTTON, S. Pupillary response at visual threshold. *Nature*, 1966, *212*, 485-486.

HESS, E. H., & POLT, J. M. Pupil size in relation to mental activity during simple problem-solving. *Science*, 1964, *140*, 1190-1192.

JAMES, W. *The principles of psychology*. New York: Dover, 1890.

JANISSE, M. P. (Ed.). *Pupillary dynamics and behavior*. New York: Plenum, 1974.

KAHNEMAN, D. *Attention and effort*. Englewood Cliffs, N.J.: Prentice-Hall, 1973.

KAHNEMAN, D., & BEATTY, J. Pupil diameter and load on memory. *Science*, 1966, *154*, 1583-1585.

KAHNEMAN, D., & BEATTY, J. Pupillary responses in a pitch-discrimination task. *Perception & Psychophysics*, 1967, *2*, 101–105.

KAHNEMAN, D.; TURSKY, B.; SHAPIRO, D., & CRIDER, A. Pupillary, heart rate, and skin resistance changes during a mental task. *Journal of Experimenal Psychology*, 1969, *79*, 164–167.

KARLIN, L. Cognition, preparation, and sensory evoked potentials. *Psychological Bulletin*, 1970, *73*, 122–136.

KELLAWAY, P., & PETERSEN, I. (Eds.). *Automation of clinical electro-encephalography.* New York: Raven, 1973.

LINDSLEY, D. B. Attention, consciousness, sleep, and wakefulness. In J. Field (Ed.), *Handbook of physiology* (Vol. 3). Washington, D.C.: American Physiological Society, 1960.

LOEWENFELD, I. E. Mechanisms of reflex dilations of the pupil. *Documenta Ophthalmologica*, 1958, *12*, 185–359.

McCALLUM, W. C., & KNOTT, J. R. (Eds.). *Event-related slow potentials of the brain: Their relations to behavior.* Amsterdam: Elsevier, 1973.

MACKWORTH, J. F. *Vigilance and habituation.* Baltimore: Penguin, 1969.

MACKWORTH, J. F. *Vigilance and attention.* Baltimore: Penguin, 1970.

MORAY, N. *Listening and attention.* Middlesex, England: Penguin, 1969. (a)

MORAY, N. *Attention: Selective processes in vision and hearing:* London: Hutchinson Educational, 1969. (b)

MORUZZI, G., & MAGOUN, H. W. Brain stem reticular formation and activation of the EEG. *Electroencephalography and Clinical Neurophysiology*, 1949, *1*, 455–473.

MOSTOFSKY, D. I. (Ed.). *Attention: Contemporary theory and analysis.* New York: Appleton-Century-Crofts, 1970.

NORMAN, D. A. *Memory and attention.* New York: Wiley, 1976.

NORMAN, D. A., & BOBROW, D. G. On data-limited and resource-limited processes. *Cognitive Psychology*, 1975, *7*, 44–64.

PAYNE, D. T.; PARRY, M. E.; & HARASYMIW, S. J. Percentage pupillary dilation as a measure of item difficulty. *Perception & Psychophysics*, 1968, *4*, 139–143.

PICTON, T. W., & HILLYARD, S. A. Human auditory evoked potentials, II: Effects of attention. *Electroencephalography and Clinical Neurophysiology*, 1974, *36*, 191–199.

POSNER, M. I. Psychobiology of attention. In M. S. Gazzaniga & C. Blakemore (Eds.), *Handbook of psychobiology*. New York: Academic Press, 1975.

RECHTSCHAFFEN, A., & KALES, A. *Manual of standardized terminology, techniques, and scoring system for sleep stages of human subjects*. U.S. Public Health Service. Washington, D.C.: U.S. Government Printing Office, 1968.

SCHWARTZ, G. E., & BEATTY, J. *Biofeedback: Theory and research*. San Francisco: Academic Press, 1977.

STROH, C. M. *Vigilance: The problem of sustained attention*. Oxford: Pergamon Press, 1971.

SWETS, J., & KRISTOFFERSON, A. B. Attention. *Annual Review of Psychology*, 1970, *21*, 339–366.

TECCE, J. J. Attention and evoked potentials in man. In D. I. Mostofsky (Ed.), *Attention: Contemporary theory and analysis*. New York: Appleton-Century-Crofts, 1970.

TECCE, J. J. Contingent negative variation (CNV) and psychological processes in man. *Psychological Bulletin*, 1972, *77*, 73–108.

TREISMAN, A. M. Strategies and models of selective attention. *Psychological Review*, 1969, *76*, 282–299.

WILLIAMS, H. L.; GRANDA, A. M.; JONES, R. C.; LUBIN, A.; & ARMINGTON, J. C. EEG frequency and finger pulse volume as predictors of reaction time during sleep loss. *Electroencephalography and Clinical Neurophysiology*, 1962, *14*, 64–70.

II

The Hemispheric Processes of the Brain

4

Review
of the Split Brain
by Michael S. Gazzaniga

One of the most interesting recent research findings about the human brain is that its two hemispheres function differently in important ways. The nature of these different functions has been intensively studied since the 1950s by biologists, psychologists, neurologists, and surgeons. One of the pioneers among these researchers is Dr. Michael S. Gazzaniga, a psychologist at the State University of New York at Stony Brook. In the following chapter he summarizes the findings about the hemispheric processes of the brain which have emerged from research in which connections between the hemispheres have been severed, resulting in so-called split brains.

The corpus callosum, the cerebral **commissure** that interconnects the left and right half-brains, was considered an enigma to neurologists and neurosurgeons in the 1940s and '50s. It was the structure discussed most often when an example was sought to show how little was known about the brain. Even though it is the largest nerve tract in the brain—which in man contains more than 200 million neurons—it was generally believed it could be sectioned and destroyed and have no apparent consequences for behavior. In fact, many quips made the rounds of medical circles about the general lack of importance of the forebrain commissures.

It was in this context that the original experiments on the split brain were carried out on the cat by Ronald Myers and Roger Sperry at the University of Chicago in the early '50s. After Myers had successfully developed the technique of splitting the optic chiasm, thereby allowing visual information presented to the right eye to be exclusively projected to the right hemisphere and visual information presented to the left eye to be exclusively projected to the left hemisphere, he discovered in follow-up behavioral tests that there was, nonetheless, **interocular** transfer. In order to determine whether one could block interhemispheric transfer of visual information, the next logical structure to section surgically was the corpus callosum. The now-classic split-brain experiments first performed on the cat showing that discriminations trained to one side of the brain leave the other half of the brain naive were the direct result of this surgical procedure. Later studies carried out in both the monkey and chimp confirmed these findings.

Still, these results stood in marked contrast to the earlier findings of Akelaitis, who had studied a series of some twenty-six patients with the corpus callosum and **anterior** commissure sectioned (cut) in complete or in part in order to achieve interhemispheric control of epileptic seizures. In an extensive series of studies, he purported to show that sectioning of these structures did not result in any significant neurological or psychological effects. He did make this point, and his view emerged as the dominant one even though there were several contradictory reports in the literature about showing disconnection effects as a result of the callosum having been sectioned or put out of order through a tumor or the like (Geschwind, 1965). At the time it was also generally considered that cutting the callosum did not, in fact, help control epilepsy.

In 1960 Dr. Joseph Bogen, then a resident at White Memorial Hospital in Los Angeles, proposed, after careful review of the Akelaitis literature, that the brain be split for the purpose of controlling the interhemispheric spread of epilepsy. The conclusion he reached—that surgery should achieve this control—proved largely correct. Along with Roger Sperry at Caltech, I devised a host of psychological tests which we administered to W. J., Dr. Bogen's first patient who was studied extensively, both pre- and postoperatively (Gazzaniga, Bogen, & Sperry, 1962, 1963, 1965; Gazzaniga & Sperry, 1967). Subsequent examination of patients in the Bogen series revealed a variety of striking and dramatic effects.

INFORMATION EXCHANGE
BETWEEN CEREBRAL HEMISPHERES

The first important finding was that the interhemispheric exchange of information was totally disrupted following **commissurotomy**. The effect was such that visual, **tactual, proprioceptive**, auditory, and olfactory information presented to one hemisphere could be processed and dealt with in that half-brain, but each of these activities went on *outside* the realm of awareness of the other half-cerebrum. This observation confirmed the animal work done earlier by Myers and Sperry, except that in a sense the results were more dramatic. Since it is the left hemisphere that normally possesses the natural language and speech mechanisms, all processes ongoing in the left hemisphere could easily be verbally described by the patients; information presented to the right hemisphere went undescribed. It was only through the use of special testing techniques developed for this purpose that we were able to discover that the right hemisphere has a rich mental life of its own and is capable of experiencing most of the activities the left brain is able to experience.

MENTAL PROPERTIES

OF THE RIGHT HEMISPHERE

We used nonverbal tests especially designed for these experiments and determined that the right hemisphere has some language, can initiate its own response, and can emote, learn, remember, and do all the things that are part of normal life without the left hemisphere knowing the why or what of it. Thus, for example, a word could be flashed in the left visual field which, in man, is exclusively projected to the right hemisphere — the word *spoon* in this instance — and the subject would say, "I did not see anything." Subsequently, with the left hand, he would be able to retrieve an object from a series of objects placed out of view. When the subject was holding the correct object in his hand and out of view the experimenter asked, "What is it you have in your hand?" and the patient answered, "I don't know." Thus again, it was proven that the left hemisphere does not know. The left hemisphere did not see the picture flashed to the right hemisphere nor did it have access to the stereognostic or touch information from the left hand which is also exclusively projected to the right hemisphere. Yet clearly, the right hemisphere recognized the word *spoon* because it reacted appropriately to the correct stimulus and made the appropriate response.

Patients such as these allow for even further studies that permit the examiner to investigate the separate mental properties of the two half-brains. We showed that the left hemisphere, as would have been predicted from early clinical reports, excelled in verbal processing of information of all kinds. The right hemisphere, however, proved superior in managing visual spatial tasks such as drawing cubes and arranging blocks to match a design. This distribution of mental work in the brain highlights a major difference between man and animals and, at the same time, raises the intriguing possibility that various modes of consciousness have separate physical identities in the brain.

The results thus obtained from earlier experiments carried out on Bogen's series of patients have been confirmed and extended to the patients of Dr. Donald Wilson at the Dartmouth Medical School. Wilson, although using a different surgical approach from Bogen, also carried out both complete and partial commissurotomies with the aim of preventing interhemispheric spread of epileptic seizures. Neuropschylogical postoperative examinations of these patients confirmed many of the earlier findings of the Bogen series. Briefly, they pointed out that visual, tactual, auditory, and olfactory information cannot be transferred following forebrain commissurotomy. Moreover, the partially sectioned cases showed that it is possible to make a surgical leison which will block visual—but not tactile—information from transferring between the two half-brains, and vice versa. Interestingly, it may not matter which part of the callosum is intact in order to realize transfer of what might be called the superordinate function of the two half-brains. In other words, the specialized activities of the right may come to the aid of the left no matter what part of the callosum is intact. However, more specific information from the right half-brain, such as visual information in the left field, cannot be communicated to the left hemisphere if the **splenium** alone is sectioned.

In our past studies of impaired brain function in patients, the particular amount of language and mental activity discovered in the right brain was thought to be the product of early brain damage. It is well known that if brain damage occurs in a young child, a bilateralization of the language and speech mechanisms results. Here it is of interest to note that there was a report in the 1970s of a patient who, at the age of 70, suffered vascular disease which specifically affected the splenium. The result of this patient's illness was bilateralization of his visual functions and a showing of the same degree of language talents that were outlined earlier in the Bogen series of patients. This kind of evidence may hint at some redundancy in the system during the normal developmental process—a redundancy which suggests that all language and all spatial functions are not strictly and exclusively lateralized to the respective left and right hemispheres.

Educational Significance

Indeed, one of the intriguing possibilities deriving from split-brain research is the possibility that man can be explicitly specialized in a variety of aspects of mental life: superiority in the verbal area might not necessarily mean superiority in the visual-spatial area—while the reverse may also hold true. If this proves correct, it may well follow that a particular child might be able to solve a problem using verbal symbols with greater ease than using visual-spatial ones, while another child might be better off solving the same problem using visual-spatial relations.

The motivational aspect of this observation, of course, cannot be overemphasized. When a child's talents lie in visual-spatial relations and he or she is being forced into a curriculum that emphasizes the verbal articulatory modes of solving a conceptual problem, this child will encounter enormous frustration and difficulty which may well result in hostility toward the teacher and, worse, toward the learning process itself. If the teacher were to be made aware that the child is specialized in visual-spatial skills and the same conceptual problem is introduced, both the discouragement and the subsequent hostility might be avoided if the child is allowed to use his special talents. Conversely, the child with high verbal skills may quite frequently be unable to visualize the spatial aspect of an assigned task; in this case also, far better results could be obtained if he is not forced into academic areas for which he is not naturally equipped.

In this regard, of course, the more we understand about the brain and the more we understand about the various kinds of cognitive processing systems we use in our normal mental life, the more clearly we can understand the components of what is normally called "intelligent behavior." We have developed an animal model for intelligence which emphasizes the importance of the short-term-memory system. A test can be designed which is able to produce, when combined with particular surgical lesions, short-term-memory deficits which have the result of making the animal appear less intelligent than his cage mates. In fact, what is at stake is merely how many variables the animal can keep in mind in a given space of time. The exciting aspect of a test of this kind is that it operationalizes the quantity of intelligence; as these tests develop, they can be specifically designed to diagnose a particular individual. Our aim is to develop a series of tests which will diagnose an individual with respect to his specific mental skills. It is more than likely that we will find that many people may be spatially bright while they are verbally dull, or spatially dull and verbally bright. Or, when dealing with certain kinds of symbols, we will find that some of us have a better short-term-memory system, some a faster processing capacity. Once these specific capacities have been identified, they will obviously be of great benefit to education: a teacher thus informed will be enormously aided in knowing how best to present materials to his or her class and obtain speedy comprehension and proficient use of these materials.

Philosophical Implications

I would like to conclude this article with a general note about split-brain research. It has been revealed that a surgeon's knife can alter the brain to produce a state which can best be described as allowing for the doubling of consciousness. This kind of research encourages us to think in terms of modes of consciousness. We must now assume that what writers, poets, and scientists have been telling us for centuries is true. The only diference between the normal and the split brain is that, due to the callosum, the normal-brain subject can switch between the various modes of consciousness, while the split-brain subject experiences a real decoupling.

I would like to add that the future of this field is beckoning and wrought with extraordinary potentialities: consider that if we study the cerebral commissure which gives us our normal state of conscious unity and we grow to comprehend its neurophysiological and neuroanatomical mechanisms more fully, we might well move closer to grasping how neurological systems encode psychological information. If we came to a clear understanding of that process, we would be a lot closer to breaking the code of the brain.

*   *   *

GAZZANIGA, M. S., BOGEN, J. E. & SPERRY, R. W. Laterality effects in somesthesis following cerebral commissurotomy in man. *Neuropsychologia* 1963, *1*, 209-215.

GAZZANIGA, M. S.; BOGEN, J. E.; & SPERRY, R. W. Observations in visual perception after disconnection of the cerebral hemispheres in man. *Brain*, 1965, *88*, 221.

GAZZANIGA, M. S.; BOGEN, J. E.; SPERRY, R. W. Some functional effects of sectioning cerebral commissures in man. *PNAS*, 1962, *48*, 1765.

GAZZANIGA, M. S., & SPERRY, R. W. Language after section of the cerebral commissure. *Brain*, 1967, *90*, 131.

GESCHWIND, N. Disconnection syndromes in animal and man. *Brain*, 1965, *88*, 237-585.

5

Man's So-called
Minor Hemisphere

by Robert D. Nebes

In man, the right cerebral hemisphere has long been referred to as the *minor* hemisphere. This is a reflection of the belief that, since language skills are organized primarily in the left hemisphere, it is this hemisphere that is dominant for most higher mental functions. This view, however, greatly underestimates the importance of the cognitive operations carried out by the right hemisphere. Dr. Robert D. Nebes, Ph.D., of the Duke University Medical Center Department of Psychiatry, describes recent research findings that have greatly changed previous conceptions of the right hemisphere and its functions, including how it relies more on imagery than language and how it processes information synthetically rather than analytically.

Since the 1950s, there has been an enormous change in our concept of the role the right cerebral hemisphere plays in higher mental activities. For most of the preceding century, the focus of scientific attention was on the left hemisphere, as it was this hemisphere which was first found to possess a cognitive function unique to it. This function, present only in the left hemisphere, is language. Given the prevailing view that it is our capacity for language which sets us apart from the lower species, it seemed logical that the hemisphere in which the comprehension and production of language takes place should be the more highly developed, and thus in ultimate control over the rest of the brain. The left was therefore called the "major," "dominant," or "leading" hemisphere, while the right was the "minor" or "subordinate" hemisphere. The prevailing theory for many years was that, while the right hemisphere might be capable of preliminary analysis of sensory information and the direction of simple motor acts, all higher mental functions either were carried out in the left hemisphere or were under its direct supervision. Even today, some neurophysiologists cling to the view that the right hemisphere is a mere unconscious automation, while we *live* in our left hemisphere.

Over the years, however, an increasing number of reports on specific cognitive deficits following right-hemispheric injury led most investigators to realize that they had underestimated the so-called minor hemisphere. This was paralleled by a change in psychologists' concepts of the nature of intelligence. In most of the original measures of intelligence, language was involved both in the presentation of the test material and in the types of mind processes tested. By the 1940s, multifactor theories of intelligence stressing the diversity of cognitive skills had been proposed and tests of nonverbal abilities devised. This eventually led to the discovery of right-hemispheric dominance on many types of tasks and the subsequent replacement of the concept of hemispheric *dominance* by one of hemispheric *specialization*. The research emphasis then shifted to discovering how the various higher mental processes are parcelled out between the two hemispheres. Starting as a crude listing of the cognitive deficits that were found to follow damage to one or the other side of the brain, neuropsychological research has now progressed to attempts to tease out the underlying psychological variables which distinguish the operations of the two cerebral hemispheres.

Three major approaches have been used to study the distribution of the various mental functions between the right and left hemispheres. The first, and to date most productive, has been to compare groups of unilaterally (one side) brain-damaged patients (Benton, 1968). The rationale is that if patients with damage restricted to their right hemisphere do worse on a task than do those with damage restricted to their left hemisphere, then right-hemisphere processes must be more vitally involved in the performance of this task than are those of the left. The second approach (Levy, 1972; Nebes, 1974) uses patients in whom, in order to control epilepsy, the major neural connections between the two hemispheres have been severed (commissurotomy). As in all humans, stimuli presented to the left of center in their visual field, or to their left hand or ear, project directly to the right hemisphere, and vice versa for right-sided stimuli; in these patients, however, the information cannot cross to the other hemisphere as it does in normal subjects, and so it is possible to compare within a single individual the abilities of the right and left hemispheres on the same task. The third approach (White, 1969) uses normal individuals and, as with commissurotomy patients, compares the subject's ability to handle stimuli on the right and left sides. Here, since the neural cross-connections are intact, the tasks must be made very difficult in order to demonstrate any difference in the efficiency with which the two hemispheres process information.

Early studies on unilaterally brain-damaged patients showed two major classes of cognitive deficits to be more prevalent after right- than after left-hemispheric injury. These were (1) a difficulty in perceiving, manipulating, and remembering the spatial relationships of objects, both to one another and to the patient himself; and (2) a difficulty in perceiving and remembering visual, tactile, and auditory stimuli which are complex, fragmentary, or hard to label and describe verbally. I will first summarize briefly the results of experiments run both on brain-damaged and on normal subjects studying these phenomena, and will then give some of the present theories on the nature of the fundamental psychological processes underlying these results.

Spatial disorientation is one of the most dramatic symptoms to follow right-hemispheric injury. Patients easily become lost even in familiar surroundings; simple mazes baffle them; they can no longer describe well-known routes, use or draw maps; they misjudge the size, distance, and direction of objects; they cannot match or copy accurately the slant of a line or the position of a dot on a page; they cannot copy simple shapes such as a four-pointed star, nor can they arrange blocks or sticks to form a required pattern. These difficulties are not restricted to vision, but occur also when the patients use their sense of touch. While such symptoms are not present in all patients with right-hemispheric injury, they are much more common than after left-hemispheric damage. This apparent lateralization of a sense of spatial relationships to the right hemisphere has been confirmed by experiments on normal subjects showing the right hemisphere to be better than the left at judging the slant of a line or the position of a dot; that is, normal subjects are faster and more accurate with such stimuli if the stimuli are presented in the left visual field, which projects to the right hemisphere. In commissurotomized patients, this right-hemispheric superiority is seen on such tasks as determining the orientation of a line or the direction of a movement of a dot.

Spatial disorientation is accentuated in unilaterally brain-damaged subjects by tasks which require either the recall or mental manipulation of spatial relationships. Thus, subjects with injury to the right hemisphere are often poor at remembering the slope of a line, the size of a gap, or the position of a dot on a line. They also do poorly on tasks in which they have to judge how a pattern would look from a spatial position other than that which they actually physically occupy, or which require them to mentally rotate a shape in order to determine whether it is identical to another shape or is its mirror image. Commissurotomized patients show this right-hemisphere preeminence on a test in which they have to determine whether a given exploded two-dimensional layout of a three-dimensional shape actually represents a given object.

Besides simple spatial interrelationships, other stimulus materials which right-hemisphere-damaged patients have difficulty perceiving and remembering include faces, unfamiliar and complex shapes for which there are no ready names, drawings of objects in which part of the contour is missing, music, and other nonverbal sounds. Again confirmatory evidence is found in normal subjects indicative of the vital role the right hemisphere plays in processing such material. Normal individuals are faster and more accurate in recognizing faces, inverted numbers, Gothic lettering, patterns of stimuli, and complex shapes when they appear in the half-field from which the right hemisphere gets its visual information. They are also better at recognizing and remembering melodies and chords presented to the left ear and thus going to the right hemisphere. This is in striking contrast to results achieved with verbal material; there they do better in the visual field or ear projecting to the left hemisphere. Commissurotomized patients also excel with faces and nonverbalizable visual or tactile stimuli if they are presented to the "minor" hemisphere.

There are several different ways to characterize the psychological properties common to tests which differentiate the capacities of the right and left hemispheres. Some investigators stress the importance of the type of response required from the subject—that is, talking or writing versus drawing, pointing, or manipulating objects. When commissurotomy patients are put in a situation in which both hemispheres are attempting to express themselves, the type of response required determines which hemisphere will predominate: if the subject has to describe or name, his left hemisphere wins out; if he has to point, his right one does. Another theory of hemispheric specialization proposes that the vital factor is the type of stimulus material. The left hemisphere is seen as handling best those tasks in which the stimuli are familiar and verbal in nature, or easily described or labeled verbally, while the right hemisphere excels on tasks involving meaningless shapes or spatial relationships which are too complex or similar to describe or distinguish in words.[7]

Other hemispheric dichotomies have been based on postulated differences in the type of information processing employed by the two sides of the brain (Bever, 1975; Bogen, 1969; Levy, 1974). This distinction between the left and right hemispheres has been described as: symbolic versus visual-spatial, associative versus apperceptive, propositional versus appositional, and analytic versus gestalt. All of these dichotomies suggest that the organization and processing of data by the right hemisphere is in terms of complex wholes, the minor hemisphere having a predisposition for perceiving the total rather than the parts. By contrast, the left hemisphere is seen to analyze input sequentially, abstracting out the relevant details and associating these with verbal symbols.

One of the first indications that the two hemispheres might differ in their basic approach to problems came from studies which noted that the drawings made by patients with right-hemispheric damage (and having an intact left hemisphere) tended to be full of details but disarticulated, with no coherent organization, while those made by patients with left-hemispheric damage (and an intact right hemisphere) had the correct overall configuration, but were greatly oversimplified, with few details. This suggests that the right hemisphere is more interested in the interrelationships of the parts of a stimulus to the whole than it is in the parts, or details, themselves. In commissurotomy patients, more evidence of this holistic bias (i.e., concern with the whole) on the part of the minor hemisphere has been found, with the right hemisphere surpassing the left at constructing from partial or fragmented sensory information a concept of the total stimulus. This was seen on tasks which required the subjects to estimate, from a small piece of an arc, the size of the complete circle from which it had come, or to visualize the complete contour of a shape from examination of its scattered fragments.

Experiments on normal subjects have shown the two cerebral hemispheres to differ even in their basic means of processing sensory input. Theoretically, an array of sensory stimuli can be dealt with (i.e., identified and an appropriate response programmed) either one at a time—serial processing—or simultaneously—parallel or holistic processing. These two possibilities can be distinguished by measuring in a visual-search task the time necessary to make a decision and by then seeing whether this time lengthens with an increase in the number of items, as it should in serial processing, or is unchanged, as would be predicted in parallel processing. It has been found (Cohen, 1973) that if normal subjects are shown an array of letters and their reaction times for determining whether all the letters are the same is measured, displays falling in the right-half field (left hemisphere) are processed serially, while those in the left-half field (right hemisphere) are processed in parallel. The most likely explanation for this dissimilarity in search strategies between the two hemispheres is that there are two different ways of treating language material—verbally and visual-spatially. Thus, while the left hemsiphere goes through and sequentially transforms each letter into an internal acoustic code (i.e., names them), the right hemisphere examines all the letters simultaneously looking for a variation in shape. This interpretation is supported by the fact that when nonverbalizable shapes are presented, subjects use parallel processing in both visual fields. Other reaction-time work also fits in with this shape-versus-name bias on the part of the right and left hemispheres. Normal subjects are quicker to signal "Same" to two letters which are physically similar (A, A) if they fall in the left field, but are quicker with two letters having different shapes but the same name (A, a), in the right field. The same pattern of results has been obtained in commisurotomy patients on tasks where the subject has to pick out a picture of an object which is *similar* to a given picture. The left hemisphere tends to choose items which are similar in their use—for example, if shown a cake on a plate it might pick out a fork—while the right hemisphere selects objects unrelated in use but structurally similar—a round straw hat with a brim. Thus, again we see a different bias on the part of the two hemispheres, with the right being interested in structural similarity, the left in semantic similarity.

From the preceding findings, it is evident that the right cerebral hemisphere makes an important contribution to human performance, having functions complementary to those of the left hemisphere. The right side of the brain probably processes information differently from the left, relying more on imagery than on language, and being more synthetic and holistic than analytic and sequential in handling data. It is certainly important in perceiving spatial relationships. It also probably provides the neural basis for our ability to take the fragmentary sensory information we receive and construct from it a coherent concept of the spatial organization of the outside world—a sort of cognitive spatial map by which we plan our actions.

What else the minor hemisphere may do is still open to question. Lately, everything from creativity and imagination to the id, ESP, and cosmic consciousness have been suggested to reside in the right hemisphere. Many people are now attempting to superimpose upon the anatomical and functional duality of the brain may of the philosophical and spiritual dualisms which have fascinated man over the centuries. Given the results to date on hemispheric specialization, it seems natural to many researchers in related fields that the scientific and technological aspects of our civilization are products of the left hemisphere, while the mystical and humanistic aspects are products of the right. The right hemisphere has thus been enthusiastically embraced by counterculture groups as their side of the brain. They see in it the antithesis to an upright technological Western society, identifying its synthetic abilities with Eastern mystics' view of the interrelationship of all things (Ornstein, 1972). How well such a grafting of philosophy onto anatomy will stand up is unclear, but certainly right-hemisphere attributes will continue to be explored in the coming years and their role in the various phases of human life examined.

If there is any truth in the assertion that our culture stresses left-hemispheric skills, this is especially true of the school systems. Selection for higher education is based predominantly on the ability to comprehend and manipulate language—a fact which may help explain why it took so long for science to come to grips with right-hemisphere abilities. If the right hemisphere does indeed process data in a manner different from the left, we may be shortchanging ourselves when we educate only left-sided talents in basic schooling. Perhaps, when people speculate about an inverse relationship between scholastic achievement and creativity, they are really talking about the effect of overtraining for verbal skills at the expense of nonverbal capacities. Many problems can be solved either by analysis or synthesis; but if people are taught to habitually examine only one approach, their ability to choose the most effective and efficient answer is diminished. Increased understanding of how the minor hemisphere works will hopefully lead to better training in how to choose between and to use the skills of both hemispheres of the human brain.

* * *

BENTON, A. L. Disorders of spatial orientation. In P. J. Vinken & G. W. Bruyn (Eds.), *Handbook of clinical neurology* (Vol. 3), Amsterdam: North Holland, 1968.

BEVER, T. G. Cerebral asymmetries in humans are due to the differentiation of two incompatible processes: Holistic and analytic. *Annals of the New York Academy of Sciences*, 1975, *263*, 251-262

BOGEN, J. E. The other side of the brain, II: An appositional mind. *Bulletin of the Los Angeles Neurological Society*, 1969, *34*, 135–162.

COHEN, G. Hemispheric differences in serial versus parallel processing. *Journal of Experimental Psychology*, 1973, *97*, 349–356.

LEVY, J. Psychobiological implications of bilateral asymmetry. In S. J. Dimond & J. G. Beaumont (Eds.), *Hemispheric function in the human brain*. New York: Halsted Press, 1974.

NEBES, R. D. Hemispheric specialization in commissurotomized man. *Psychological Bulletin*, 1974, *81*, 1–14.

ORNSTEIN, R. E. *The psychology of consciousness*. San Francisco: Freeman, 1972.

WHITE, M. J. Laterality differences in perception. *Psychological Bulletin*, 1969, *72*, 387–405.

6

The Left Hemisphere
by Stephen D. Krashen

The left cerebral hemisphere, at least in most people, processes language. The left hemisphere has also been shown to process both linguistic and non-linguistic information in characteristic ways: It is analyzed, linearly arranged, temporally ordered (i. e., ordered according to time of occurrence), and represented as propositions. Dr. Stephen Krashen, a professor of linguistics at the University of Southern California, describes the verbal and nonverbal functions of the left hemisphere—how it organizes information sequentially, understands language, and produces speech. He also discusses group and individual differences in brain processes, eye movements, and cognitive style.

For most people (nearly all right-handers and many left-handers) the left hemisphere is dominant for language. Gradually, a precise characterization of dominance is emerging from an interdisciplinary group of scholars, scientists, and physicians concerned with the subject of cerebral asymmetry. It is known that the left side of the brain is somehow involved in the language function, for the following reasons:

- Loss of speech caused by brain damage occurs far more frequently from left-sided lesions than from right-sided lesions (Russell & Espir, 1961).

- When the left hemisphere is temporarily anesthetized, loss of speech results; but when the right hemisphere is anthetized, this generally does not happen (Wada & Rasmussen, 1960).

- When competing, simultaneous verbal material is presented to the two ears (a procedure called **dichotic listening**), a reliable right-ear superiority in response accuracy and reaction time is found: The stimuli presented to the right ear are more often recalled correctly and subjects can react faster to them. This right-ear advantage is presumably due to better right-ear connections to the left hemisphere (Kimura, 1961).

- When verbal material (or material easily coded into language) is presented to right and left visual fields, most subjects show a right- visual-field superiority in response accuracy and reaction time, presumably due to better right-field connections to the left hemisphere (McKeever & Huling, 1970, 1971; Umilta, Rizzolata, Marzi, Zamboni, Franzini, Camarda, Berlucchi, 1974).

- During verbal tasks, whether performance is overt or covert, researchers have found signs of greater electrical activity in the left hemisphere. This is shown by analysis of brain waves; for example, the more active side of the brain produced less "alpha," the brain wave associated with resting states (Morgan, McDonald, & MacDonald, 1971; Robbins & McAdam, 1974; Wood, Goff, & Day, 1971).

The emerging picture of cerebral dominance is a complex one: All aspects of language are not limited to the left hemisphere, and the left hemisphere appears to do more than just control language functions. Also, individuals seem to vary in at least two important ways. First, some people seem to be less lateralized than others; that is, for some subjects, language appears to be more diffusely represented in the two hemispheres, and not as confined to the left side. Second, some people may appeal to one side of the brain, the left or the right, more readily in their cognitive functioning. Below, we will examine some of the research that has led to these conclusions.

Is the Left Hemisphere Verbal?

The original discovery that language is processed primarily by the left hemisphere was made by observing the effects of unilateral brain damage. Damage to the left hemisphere, rather than to the right, was clearly associated with language disturbance. Research in cerebral asymmetry in humans was thus limited to brain-damaged subjects. Kimura (1961, 1967) discovered a safe and reliable technique that enabled researchers to use normal subjects for the study of cerebral asymmetry. This method had several advantages: Results were not confounded with the effects of brain damage, and experimenters were able to use this new technique to examine some detailed hypotheses on the relation between language and other left-hemisphere functions.

Kimura's discovery was that the dichotic-listening technique, used in experimental psychology by Broadbent for the investigation of attention, was a valid and reliable measure of cerebral asymmetry. In dichotic listening, subjects hear competing, simultaneous stimuli. For example, the left ear might hear the digit *six* while the right ear hears *two*. Kimura found that when subjects with known left-hemisphere dominance for language heard series of pairs of digits, the right ear consistently outperformed the left ear. While the right-ear advantage was not huge, it was statistically significant and reliable. Kimura suggested that the right-ear advantage was a reflection of left-brain dominance for language, a hypothesis that has been confirmed many times since Kimura's initial study. The right ear outperforms the left ear because it has better access to the left hemisphere, thanks to the superiority of the crossed auditory pathways. While the right ear connects directly to the left hemisphere, the left ear's route to the language areas must first pass through the right himisphere before "crossing over" to the left side (see Figure 6.1).

FIGURE 6.1. Model for Dichotic Listening

After Kimura's findings that dichotically presented digits produced a right-ear advantage, investigators sought to determine what other stimuli would produce a right-ear advantage. In other words, they asked what other subparts of language were processed by the left hemisphere.

Dirks (1964) extended Kimura's findings to dichotically presented words, while Curry (1967) found that both dichotic meaningful and nonsense words produced a right-ear advantage. This last result indicated that the left hemisphere is specialized not merely for linguistically meaningful stimuli. This finding was confirmed by Shankweiler and Studdert-Kennedy (1967), who reported a right-ear advantage for synthetically produced CV (consonant-vowel) syllables contrasting in the consonant segment, such as /ba/ and /ga/.

The finding that dichotically presented melodies (Kimura, 1964), sonar signals (Chaney & Webster, 1966), and environmental sounds (Curry, 1967) were better perceived by the left ear in normal, righthanded subjects dismissed any hypothesis that the left hemisphere was specialized merely for some level of audition or general attention.

Kimura (1967) tested the hypothesis that the left hemisphere was specialized for the perception of *familiar* stimuli. She presented normal, right-handed subjects with dichotic "familiar concert melodies" which could not easily be identified by name. Subjects were asked to hum the melodies afterward and state whether the melodies were familiar. A clear *left*-ear advantage was found for all melodies, even in cases where both compositions presented were familiar to the subject. This forced Kimura to conclude that "familiarity, of itself, does not appear to be a critical factor in hemispheric specialization of function" (Kimura, 1967, p. 176).

Dichotic-listening research done by members of the Haskins Laboratories has supported the hypothesis that the left hemisphere is attuned to particular aspects of speech perception, namely the *drastic restructuring* needed to decode speech. In a number of experiments (summarized in Liberman, Cooper, Shankweiler, Studdert-Kennedy, 1967), Haskins researchers have shown that there is a very indirect relationship between the acoustic speech signal and the linear succession of discrete speech segments we think we hear. For example, when we "hear" the word *big*, information about the first consonant, the /b/, may be spread out over the first two-thirds of the acoustic signal, information about the vowel may extend over the whole signal, and information about the /g/ may cover the last two-thirds of the signal. Somehow, this overlapping of acoustic cues has to be sorted out and separated. Another problem is that what is perceived as one phonetic segment may result from very different acoustic cues in different contexts; the cues for the /d/ in *dead* may be quite different from the cues for the /d/ in *duty*. (See Liberman et al. for a technical discussion of the nature of these acoustic cues.)

In other words, there is a lack of a one-to-one correspondence between phoenetic units, or the speech segments we think we hear in a linear sequence, and the acoustic cues corresponding to these units. The cues may be transmitted in parallel and may vary with context. The Haskins researchers have hypothesized that the left hemisphere is specially equipped to deal with this decoding problem.

Evidence for this hypothesis comes from dichotic-listening experiments that compare the right-ear advantage for speech sounds that require a great deal of decoding with sounds that require less decoding. It is predicted that heavily "encoded" sounds will show a greater right-ear advantage, reflecting greater use of the left hemisphere. Stop consonants (such as /b/, /d/, /g/, /p/, /t/, and /k/) demand a great deal of restructuring. Vowels, on the other hand, especially when produced in isolation, require a minimum of decoding. For such sounds, there is no parallel transmission of acoustic cues and no contextual changes in cues. The Haskins position thus received its first important confirmation with Shankweiler and Studdert-Kennedy's (1967) discovery that dichotic "steady-state" (artificially produced) vowels did not cause a right-ear advantage, while presentation of dichotic stop consonants accompanied by the vowel /a/ did give a right-ear advantage. A subsequent study (Studdert-Kennedy & Shankweiler, 1970), using natural stimuli, confirmed the right-ear advantage for consonant-contrasting CVC syllables (e.g., /bip/ versus /gip/) and furthur demonstrated the lack of a significant right-ear advantage for vowel-contrasting CVCs (e.g., /bip/ versus /bap/.)*

Haskins research has shown that the perception of fricatives, consonants such as /s/, /z/, /f/, and /v/, is partially dependent on acoustic cues that require restructuring and partially dependent on cues that do not require extensive decoding. Darwin's (1971) study confirmed the Haskins hypothesis that the left hemisphere is specialized for restructuring when he demonstrated that dichotic fricatives produced a right-ear advantage just when those cues were present that required restructuring. Fricatives synthesized

*The right-ear advantage has been produced for vowel stimuli under various conditions, for example, when the vowels are embedded in noise (Weiss & House, 1973), and when the duration of the stimulus is shortened (Godfrey, 1974).

and presented dichotically with invariant cues were identifiable by Darwin's subjects, but no right-ear advantage was found.

Similarly, Cutting (1972) found that liquid consonants (/r/ and /l/) and semivowels (/y/ and /w/) produce a right-ear advantage that is greater than that found for vowels but less than that found for stop consonants. This also confirms the Haskins hypothesis, as liquids and semivowels demand less decoding than do stop consonants but more decoding than do vowels. Cutting suggested that there exists "an ear effect continuum which parallels an encodedness continuum" (p. 61), with stop consonants being the most encoded and showing the largest right-ear advantage in dichotic listening, and with vowels the least encoded and showing the least right-ear advantage.

While these results strongly confirm the hypothesis that the left hemisphere contains a device designed especially for the perception of the speech code, less obviously encoded subparts of language have been shown to be dependent on left-hemisphere mechanisms as well.

Evidence has been found that the grammatical structure of sentences is analyzed best by the left hemisphere (Zurif & Sait, 1969), as well as linguistic tone. In some languages, like Thai, the pitch a word is spoken on may change the meaning of the word. For example, the Thai word /náa/, spoken with a high tone, means "aunt," but the Thai word /n$\overline{aa}$/, spoken with a lower tone, means "field." Van Lancker and Fromkin (1973) have found that Thai speakers show a right-ear advantage for dichotically presented syllables differing only in linguistic tone, indicating that the left hemispere may be specialized for *linguistic processing,* since tones presented to the same subjects in a nonlinguistic context (hummed without an accompanying syllable) did not give a right-ear advantage. (This latter result is consistent with studies that show no lateralization for nonlinguistic pitch perception; Doehling, 1972; Curry, 1968.)

Further evidence that the left hemisphere's task includes the purely linguistic function is the finding by Gordon and Carmon

(1976). In their experiment, subjects identified symbols for which they had just learned verbal labels (digits), such as dots representing binary numbers. As the experiment progressed, subjects showed a shift from right-hemisphere processing (left-visual-field superiority) to left-hemisphere processing (right-visual-field superiority). Gordon and Carmon suggest that the left hemisphere's advantage "for naming or codifying produced the reversal" (p. 1097). As the subjects learned the names of the symbols they saw, the left hemisphere played a larger role in their identification.

The above discussion has indicated that not all aspects of language are processed exclusively by the left hemisphere (e.g., certain cues for fricatives and vowels); it may also be the case that the right hemisphere is involved in some parts of normal language processing. Blumstein and Cooper (1974) found a left-ear advantage in normal, right-handed subjects for the identification of intonation contours (corresponding to the intonation used for declarative, imperative, conditional, and interrogative sentences in English), even when such contours were superimposed on linguistic material (a series of short nonsense syllables). This result contrasts with Van Lancker and Fromkin's results with linguistic tone, but, as Blumstein and Cooper point out, it is consistent with observations that left-hemisphere damage does not seem to affect recognition of intonation: **Aphasics**—brain-damaged (usually left) patients with partial or complete loss of language—can often distinguish commands, questions, and declarative sentences. Blumstein and Cooper conclude that "the right hemisphere is directly involved in the processing of intonation contours . . . (and) normal language perception may involve the simultaneous analysis of the linguistic input in both hemispheres" (p. 156). It would be interesting to discover whether nonaphasic right-himisphere-damaged patients display any sort of inability to produce or perceive intonation contours. (See Zurif, 1974, for comments on the Blumstein & Cooper study.)

Not only is there evidence of normal language processing in

the right hemisphere, but there is also good evidence that a great deal of nonverbal processing occurs in the left hemisphere. Most of these nonverbal left-hemisphere functions appear to be *time-related,* and include the following:

- *The ability to do fine temporal-order judgments (e.g., judging which of two stimuli comes first):* Evidence for this includes Carmon and Nachson's (1971) report that patients with left lesions performed worse than controls and right-lesioned patients in tasks involving the temporal order of rapid, repeated sequences of colored lights and sounds. Papcun, Krashen, Terbeek, Remington, and Harshman (1974) found that dichotically presented Morse code signals produced a right-ear advantage for both experienced Morse code operators and subjects who did not know the code. Since the perception of Morse code requires judgments of the temporal order of the individual dots and dashes, this result also confirms that temporal-order judgments are lateralized to the left hemisphere. (see also Halperin, Nachshon, & Carmon, 1973.)

- *Simultaneity judgments:* Efron (1963) found that subjects reported that identical light and tactile stimuli presented to opposite side of the body were perceptually simultaneous when the left-sided stimulus preceded the right-sided stimulus by about 3 milliseconds. The earlier onset necessary for the left-sided stimulus is consistent with the hypothesis that simultaneity is judged in the left hemisphere, the left-sided stimulus having a longer pathway than the right-sided one to the left hemisphere, as it must first proceed along crossed pathways to the right hemisphere.

- *Temporal resolution:* Lackner and Teuber (1973) found that patients with left lesions required longer interstimulus intervals to perceive two clicks as separate entities than right-hemisphere-damaged and control subjects.

- *Programming rapid motor sequences:* Hécaen (1962) has presented extensive evidence that "ideomotor apraxia," a disorder described by Williams (1970) as "the loss of skilled sequences," results primarily from lesions of the left hemisphere, and especially the parietal lobe. Kimura and Vanderwolf (1970) found a *left*-hand superiority in right-handed normal subjects for the flexion of individual and pairs of fingers, suggesting that "the peculiar contribution of the left hemisphere to manual skill may thus consist, not in increased discreteness of movement (fractionalization), but in the increased efficiency with which individual movements can be coordinated into a sequence" (p. 775). More recently, Kimura and Archibald (1974) found left-lesioned subjects to be impaired on tasks requiring "unfamiliar meaingless movements of the hand and arm" (p. 349), as well as in tasks requiring the use of familiar objects, relative to right-damaged patients. There was no correlation between performance on this motor-sequencing task and performance on a finger-flexion task, indicating their reliance on separate systems in the brain.

The various abilities of the left hemisphere may perhaps be generalized further. On the basis of the performance of split-brain subjects (see Chapter 5 by Dr. Nebes in this book) on a task involving matching three-dimensional forms to visually expanded forms, Levy-Agresti and Sperry (1968) conclude that "the mechanisms used by the two hemispheres in solving the problems appeared to be different. . . . the data indicate that the mute, minor hemisphere is specialized for Gestalt perception, being primarily a synthesist in dealing with information input. The speaking, major hemisphere, in contrast, seems to operate in a more logical, analytic, computer-like fashion" (p. 1151).

Bever and Chiarello (1974) have also presented evidence that supports the hypothesis that the left hemisphere is basically an analytic processor. Monaural melodies were presented both to musically sophisticated listeners, who characteristically listen to music in an analytic fashion, focusing on the relations of the individual notes to each other, and to musically naive subjects, who "focus on the overall contour of the melody" (p. 539). It was found that the experienced listeners showed a right-ear advantage for melody recognition, while the inexperienced listeners showed a left-ear advantage. Bever and Chiarello conclude that their results are consistent with the hypothesis that the left hemisphere is specialized for "internal stimulus analysis" (p. 539).

The finding that the left hemisphere is specialized for non-linguistic as well as linguistic functions leads to the question of the relationship of the language function to the nonlinguistic functions. Language production and perception are of course heavily dependent on the temporal capacities of the brain; temporal-order judgments are necessary in syntax, where grammatical relations are often signaled by the order of units—what is essentially involved in language production is the programming of an idea, itself containing no intrinsic temporal order, into a sequence of linguistic units, which are also intrinsically unordered. The analysis-by-synthesis model (Neisser, 1967) implies that similar processing is involved in speech perception.

It is thus possible that the language faculty is "attracted, in most of us, to the left rather than the right side because of a pre-existing advantage in temporal acuity of the left hemisphere" (Lackner & Teuber, 1973, p. 413). Left-hemisphere specialization for language may thus actually be a result of left-hemisphere specialization for more "primary" mental abilities (Krashen, 1973b).

Several interesting possibilities follow from this hypothesis. First, as mentioned above, some aspects of language may be localized in the right hemisphere. These would be aspects that rely less on the analytic properties of the left hemisphere. Second, all languages need not be equally lateralized to the left. Some languages may rely more on left-hemisphere mental abilities than others. For suggestive evidence, see Rogers, TenHouten, Kaplan,

and Gardiner (1976), who report greater left-hemisphere localization for English than for Hopi.

The Development
of the Left Hemisphere

There is, at present, some controversy over the issue of the
development of cerebral dominance. Leeneberg (1967) argued
that the infant's brain is not firmly specialized, and that the adult
level of lateralization is established by around puberty. Krashen
(1973a) presented evidence that indicated that lateralization is
accomplished much earlier, by around age five (see also Krashen
& Harshman, 1972; Dorman & Geffner, 1974; Berlin, Hughes,
Lowe-Bell, & Berlin, 1973; Hécaen, 1976). More recently, clear
signs of hemispheric asymmetry have been shown to be present
in newborns and very young children (Molfese, 1972; Gardiner,
Schulman, & Walter, 1973; Witelson & Pallie, 1974; Caplan &
Kinsbourne, 1976; Wada, Clarke, & Hamm, 1975), and Kinsbourne (1975) has argued that, in fact, there is no development of
cerebral dominance at all: Language is lateralized to the left
hemisphere from the start. Finally, Krashen (1975) has maintained
that the above studies are all consistent with the hypothesis that
while signs of the beginning of the development of cerebral dominance are present at birth, the adult level is achieved by age five.

The "age five" position is consistent with the hypothesis that
the processes of first-language acquisition and the development
of cerebral dominance are related, as the fundamental parts of
first-language acquisition are also complete by around five.
Krashen and Harshman (1972) have suggested that the acquisition
of language may involve, and depend on, the cerebral lateralization of certain crucial functions, possibly the time-related mental
abilities discussed above. Consistent with this view are findings

that children over five who exhibit deficits in linguistic development (**dyslexics,** or poor readers) do not show the adult level of cerebral dominance when tested by dichotic listening (Zurif & Carson, 1970; Taylor, in Kimura, 1967; Thomson, 1976).Also, children who suffer from retarded language show deficits in temporal processing (Lowe & Campbell, 1965; Poppen, Stark, Eisonson, Forrest, & Wertheim, 1969; Tallal & Piercy, 1974; Corkin, 1974).

Group Differences in Degree of Lateralization

Certain individuals never attain the adult level of cerebral specialization of functions. Also, it has been suggested (Geffner & Hochberg, 1971; see also Borowy & Goebel, 1976) that environmental deprivation may slow down the normal course of the development of cerebral dominance; most cases of incomplete dominance, however, or diffuse representation of what "should be" lateralized functions appear in members of one or both of two oft-maligned but less obviously deprived groups: left-handers and women.

It is estimated that about two-thirds of all left-handers are lateralized like right-handers, with language and other time-related functions localized in the left hemisphere. The other one-third, however, may have right-hemisphere language or some degree of diffuse representation (Milner, Branch, & Rasmussen, 1964). Those left-handers who have right-hemisphere localization of language present a problem for any theory that language and the time-related functions are related. If the basis for handedness is the superiority in the performance of rapid motor sequences with one hand, as suggested by Kimura and Vanderwerf, such individuals will have the motor-sequencing ability localized in the nonlanguage hemisphere. These cases make it difficult to argue for a necessary relationship between the sequencing ability and the language function for all humans.

There has been limited success in characterizing individuals with reversed dominance—language represented in the right hemisphere. Several researchers have attempted to associate this phenomenon with whether the subject has a family history of left-handedness. Zurif and Bryden (1969), for example, found that left-handers with no family history of left-handedness (no left-handed parents or siblings) appeared to behave like right-handers on tests measuring language dominance: they showed left-hemisphere representation for language. Other researchers, however, claim opposite results, reporting that left-handers without a family history of left-handedness tend to have right-hemisphere representation for language (Ratcliff & Newcombe, 1973; Satz, Achenbach, & Fennell, 1967; Warrington & Pratt, 1973; see also Lake & Bryden, 1976). There have also been attempts to relate reversed dominance to strength or consistency of handedness on various tasks. Knox and Boone (1970) and Satz et al. (1967) found that "strongly" left-handed subjects tended to be right-dominant for language. Dee (1971), however, found that "strong" left-handers, like right-handers, were left dominant for language, while "moderate" left-handers showed reverse dominance.

Levy (1969) noted that left-handers (selected from a population of college students) performed significantly lower than right-handers on the WAIS (Wechster Adult Intelligence Scale) Performance Tests. Performance on this part of the WAIS is known to be relatively more dependent on the right hemisphere in right-handers: Since left-handers, as a group, are more diffusely lateralized, with both linguistic and nonlinguistic functions represented in both hemispheres, Levy hypothesized that the resulting "competition" seems to interfere with abilities usually associated with the "minor hemisphere" (p. 615). (See also Nebes, 1971; Miller, 1971; Gilbert, 1973; Nebes & Briggs, 1974.)

There is fairly clear evidence that visual-spatial skills are more clearly located in the right hemisphere for males (Kimura, 1969, 1973; Lansdell, 1962) and experiments in dichotic listening have produced evidence of greater male lateralization for some aspects of verbal processing (Harshman, Remington, & Krashen, 1974; see also Hannay & Malone, 1976; Lake & Bryden, 1976; Ray, Morell, Frediani, & Tucker, 1976). If females are indeed less lateralized than males, this may help to explain the observed superiority of males for spatial skills, as Levy's competition hypothesis predicts lowered right-hemisphere abilities in such cases.

Hemisphericity

Another interesting area of investigation concerns the intriguing possibility that individuals have a tendency to appeal to one hemisphere and its mode of thought more than the other. The indicator of such "hemisphericity" (term borrowed from Bogen, DeZure, TenHouten, & Marsh, 1972) often used in research is conjugate lateral eye movement, the tendency people have to move both eyes in one direction, either to the right or the left, when asked to reflect or compute internally. This phenomenon was first noticed by Day (1964), and he suggested (Day, 1967) that the "right mover," a person who tends to look to the right while reflecting, shows an "externalized activity responsive distribution of attention . . . (while) the left mover shows an internalized, subjective, passively verbal expressive distribution of attention" (p. 439).

Bakan (1969) has suggested that direction of eye movement is related to hemisphericity, left movements related to right-hemisphere thought and right movements related to left-hemisphere thought. Evidence for this is a series of studies that show that left lookers outperform right lookers in what seem to be "appositional" (Bogen, 1969) or right-hemisphere functions. (Left lookers report more vivid imagery, related to right-hemisphere specialization for visual-spatial functions [Bakan, 1969] and consider themselves to be more musical [Bakan, 1971] and more artistic [Harnad, 1972], while right lookers tend to better in propositional, or left-hemisphere, skills—(e.g., they score higher on the SAT mathematics subtest [Bakan, 1969], are faster in concept-identification tasks [Weitan & Etaugh, 1973], and tend to major in "hard" [science and quantitative] areas [Bakan, 1969].)

Hartnett (1974) (see also Krashen, Seliger, & Hartnett, 1974) found that "hemisphericity" may play a role in adult second-language learning. It was found that successful foreign-language students who were taught by an analytic, heavily deductive method of learning Spanish (explicit rules preceding practice) were predominately right lookers, while a group of students who were successful at a more direct, conversational, inductive approach did not have a preferred direction. This suggests that the kind of learning that took place in the second group can be achieved through either hemisphere or a combination of both.

Differences in conjugate lateral eye movement thus seem to relate to differences in cognitive or conceptual style; right lookers may be "analytic" thinkers (Cohen, 1969) and left lookers "relational" thinkers. Different approaches to learning may be optimal for each kind of thinker, or, alternatively, different strategies may need to be made available within the same—inevitably homogeneous—classroom.*

In recent years, our view of the left hemisphere has been altered by studies that reveal nonlanguage processing in the left

*Gur (1975; see also Gur, Gur, & Haris, 1975, and Kinsbourne, 1974) noted that subjects adopted a strategy of either left or right movement, independent of the question asked, when tested with the experimenter in front of them (as done in Day, Bakan, and Hartnett studies cited here). Subjects were more influenced by the type of question, however, when the experimenter stood in back (with eye movement monitored on videotape). Gur speculates that the experimenter in front condition is more anxiety-arousing, which "causes some subjects to retreat to habitual processing modes, left hemispheric for some and right hemispheric for others" (Kinsbourne, 1974, p. 280).

hemisphere as well as studies that show some aspects of normal language processing in both hemispheres or in only the right hemisphere: The language function therefore may be "overlaid" on more primary mental abilities (Krashen, 1973b). The study of the left hemisphere is thus beginning to extend beyond purely linguistic considerations — indeed, the rapidly increasing store of knowledge about the left hemisphere promises to make further contributions to the whole range of human behavior.

* * *

BAKAN, P. Hypnotizability, laterality of eye movements, and functional brain asymmetry. *Perceptual and Motor Skills*, 1969, *28*, 927-932.

BAKAN, P. The eyes have it. *Psychology Today*, 1971, *4*, 64-69.

BERLIN, C.; HUGHES, L.; Lowe-Bell, S.; & Berlin, H. Dichotic right ear advantage in children 5 to 13. *Cortex*, 1973, *9*, 393-402.

BEVER, T., & CHIARELLO, R. Cerebral dominance in musicians and non-musicians. *Science*, 1974, *185*, 537-539.

BEVER, T.; HURTIG, R.; & HANDEL, A. Analytic processing elicits right ear superiority in monaurally presented speech. *Neuropsychologia*, 1976, *14*, 175-181.

BLUMSTEIN, S. & COOPER, W. Hemispheric processing of intonation contours. *Cortex*, 1974, *10*, 146-158.

BOGEN, J. The other side of the brain II. An appositional mind. *Bulletin of the Los Angeles Neurological Societies*, 1969, *34*, 73-105.

BOGEN, U.; DeZURE, R.; TenHOUTEN, W.; & MARSH, J. The other side of the brain: The A/P ratio. *Bulletin of the Los Angeles Neurological Societies*, 1972, *37*, 49-61.

BOROWY, T., & GOEBEL, R. Cerebral lateralization of speech: The effects of sex, race, and socio-economic class. *Neuropsychologia*, 1976, *14*, 363-370.

Note that those subjects who initially look right when reflecting on a nonverbal problem (when facing the experimenter) are appealing to the "inappropriate" hemisphere for the task. They may eventually deal with the problem using the other side of the brain (Dumas & Morgan, 1976). That is, a "left-hemisphere thinker" may be someone who appeals to his left hemisphere first, and/or has relatively better developed left-hemisphere abilities. He need not, however, use the left hemisphere for all cognitive functioning.

BROWN, J., & JAFFE, J. Hypothesis on cerebral dominance. *Neuropsychologia*, 1975, *13*, 107-110.

CAPLAN, P. & KINSBOURNE, M. Baby drops the rattle: Asymmetry of duration of grasp by infants. *Child Development*, 1976, *42*, 532-534.

CARMON, A., & NACHSHON, I. Effect of unilateral brain-damage on perception of temporal order. *Cortex*, 1971, *7*, 410-418.

CHANEY, R., & WEBSTER, J. Information in certain multi-dimensional sounds. *Journal of the Acoustical Society of America*, 1966, *25*, 975-979.

COHEN, R. Conceptual styles, culture conflict, and nonverbal tests of intelligence. *American Anthropologist*, 1969, *71*, 828-856.

CORKIN, S. Serial-ordering deficits in inferior readers. *Neuropsychologia*, 1971, *12*, 347-354.

CRITCHLEY, M. Speech and speech-loss in relation to the quality of the brain. In V. Mountcastle (Ed.), *Interhemispheric relations and cerebral dominance.* Baltimore: John Hopkins Press, 1962.

CURRY, F. A comparison of left-handed and right-handed subjects on verbal and non-verbal dichotic listening tasks. *Cortex*, 1967, *3*, 343-352.

CURRY, F. A comparison of the performance of a right hemispherectomized subject and twenty-five normals on four dichotic listening tasks. *Cortex*, 1968, *4*, 144-153.

CUTTING, J. A parallel between degree of encodedness and the ear advantage: Evidence from an ear-monitoring task. *Journal of the Accoustical Society of America*, 1972, *53*, 358(A).

DARWIN, C. Ear differences in the recall of fricatives and vowels. *Quarterly Journal of Experimental Psychology*, 1971, *23*, 46-62.

DAY, M. An eye-movement phenomenon relating to attention, thought, and anxiety. *Perceptual and Motor Skills*, 1964, *19*, 443-446.

DAY, M. An eye-movement indicator of type and level of anxiety: Some clinical observations. *Journal of Clinical Psychology*, 1967, *66*, 51-62.

DEE, H. Auditory asymmetry and strength of manual preference. *Cortex*, 1971, *7*, 236-244.

DIRKS, D. Perception of dichotic and monaural verbal material and cerebral dominance in man. *Acta Otolaryng*, 1964, *58*, 73–80.

DOEHLING, D. Ear asymmetry in the discrimination of monarual tonal sequences. *Canadian Journal of Psychology*, 1972, *26*, 106–110.

DORMAN, M., & GEFFNER, D. Hemispheric specialization for speech perception in six-year-old black and white children from low and middle socioeconomic classes. *Cortex*, 1974, *10*, 171–176.

DUMAS, R., & MORGAN, A. EEG asymmetry as a function of occupation, task, and task difficulty. *Neuropsychologia*, 1975, *13*, 219–228.

EFRON, R. The effect of handedness on the perception of simultaneity and temporal order. *Brain*, 1963, *86*, 261–284.

GALIN, D., & ORNSTEIN, R. Individual differences in cognitive style, I. Reflective eye movements. *Neuropsychologia*, 1974, *12*, 367–376.

GARDINER, M; SHULMAN, C.; & WALTER, D. Facultative EEG asymmetries in babies and adults. UCLA BIS report #34, 1973, 37–40.

GEFFNER, D., & HOCHBRG, I. Ear laterality performance of children from low and middle socioeconomic levels in a verbal dichotic listening task. *Cortex*, 1971, *2*, 193–203.

GILBERT, C. Strength of left-handedness and facial recognition ability. *Cortex*, 1973, *9*, 145–151.

GODFREY, J. Perceptual difficulty and the right ear advantage for vowels. *Brain and Language*, 1974, *1*, 323–335.

GORDON, H., & CARMON, A. Transfer of dominance in speed of verbal response to visually presented stimuli from right to left hemisphere. *Perceptual and Motor Skills*, 1976, *42*, 1091–1100.

GUR, R. E. Conjugate lateral eye movement as an index of hemisphere activation. *Journal of Personality and Social Psychology*, 1975, *31*, 751–757.

GUR, R. E.; GUR, R. C.; & HARRIS, L. Cerebral activation, as measured by subjects' lateral eye movements, is influenced by experimenter location. *Neuropsychologia*, 1975, *13*, 35–44.

HALPERIN, Y.; NACHSHON, I.; & CARMON, A. Shift of ear superiority ir dichotic listening to temporally patterned nonverbal stimuli. *Journal of the Acoustical Society of America*, 1973, *53*, 46–50.

HANNAY, H., & MALONE, D. Visual field recognition for right handed females as a function of familial handedness. *Cortex*, 1976, *12*, 41–48.

HARNAD, S. Creativity, lateral saccades and the nondominant hemisphere. *Perceptual and Motor Skills*, 1972, *34*, 653–654.

HARSHMAN, R., & KRASHEN, S. On the development of lateralization. UCLA BIS report #34, 1973, 9–12.

HARSHMAN, R.; REMINGTON, R.; & KRASHEN, S. Sex, language, and the brain. Paper presented at the Neurosciences meeting, Brain Research Institute, UCLA, September 27, 1974.

HARTNETT, D. The relation of cognitive style and hemispheric preference to deductive and inductive second language learning. Paper presented at the Neurosciences meeting, Brain Research Institute, UCLA, September 27, 1974.

HÉCAEN, H. Clinical symtomology in right and left hemisphere lesions. In V. Mountcastle (Ed.), *Interhemispheric relations and cerebral dominance*. Baltimore: John Hopkins Press, 1962.

HÉCAEN, H. Acquired aphasia in children and the ontogenesis of hemispheric functional specialization. *Brain and Language*, 1976, *3*, 114–134.

HINES, D. Recognition of verbs, abstract nouns, and concrete nouns from the left and right visual half fields. *Neuropsychologia*, 1976, *14*, 211–216.

KIMURA, D. Cerebral dominance and the perception of verbal stimuli. *Canadian Journal of Psychology*, 1961, *15*, 166–171.

KIMURA, D. Left-right differences in the perception of melodies. *Quarterly Journal of Experimental Psychology*, 1964, *16*, 355–358.

KIMURA, D. Functional asymmetry of the brain in dichotic listening. *Cortex*, 1967, *3*, 163–178.

KIMURA, D. Spatial localization in left and right visual fields. *Canadian Journal of Psychology*, 1969, *23*, 445–458.

KIMURA, D. The asymmetry of the human brain. *Scientific American*, 1973, *228*, 70–78.

KIMURA, D., & ARCHIBALD, Y. Motor function of the left hemisphere. *Brain*, 1974, *97*, 337–350.

KIMURA, D., & VANDERWOLF, C. The relation between hand preference and the preference of individual finger movements by left and right hands. *Brain*, 1970, *93*, 769-774.

KINSBOURNE, M. Direction of gaze and distribution of cerebral thought processes. *Neuropsychologia*, 1974, *12*, 279-281.

KINSBOURNE, M. The ontogeny of cerebral dominance. In D. Aaronson & R. Rieber (Eds.), *Developmental psycholinguistics and communicative disorders.* New York Academy of Science, 1975.

KNOX, A., & BOONE, D. Auditory laterality and tested handedness *Cortex*, 1970, *6*, 164-173.

KRASHEN, S. Lateralization, language learning, and the critical period: Some new evidence. *Language Learning*, 1973, *23*, 63-74. (a)

KRASHEN, S. Mental abilities underlying linguistic and non-linguistic functions. *Linguistics*, 1973, *115*, 39-55. (b)

KRASHEN, S. The development of cerebral dominance and language learning: More new evidence. In D. Dato (Ed.), *Developmental psycholinguistics: Theory and applications.* Washington, D.C.: Georgetown University School of Languages and Linguistics, 1975.

KRASHEN, S. & HARSHMAN, R. Lateralization and the critical period. *UCLA Working Papers in Phonetics*, 1972, *23*, 13-21.

KRASHEN, S.; SELIGER, H.; & HARTNETT, D. Two studies in adult second language learning. *Kritikon Litterarum*, 1974, *2/3*, 220-228.

LACKNER, J., & TEUBER, H. Alterations in auditory fusion thresholds after cerebral injury in man. *Neuropsychologia*, 1973, *11*, 409-415.

LAKE, D., & BRYDEN, M. Handedness and sex differences in hemispheric asymmetry. *Brain and Language*, 1976, *3*, 266-282.

LANSDELL, H. A sex difference in effect of temporal lobe neurosurgery on design preference. *Nature*, 194, 852-854.

LENNEBERG, E. *Biological foundations of language.* New York: Wiley, 1967.

LEVY, J. Possible basis for the evolution of lateral specialization of the human brain. *Nature*, 1969, *224*, 614-615.

LEVY-AGRESTI, J., & SPERRY, R. Differential perceptual capacities in major and minor hemispheres. *Proceedings of the National Academy of Science*, 1968, *61*, 1151.

LIBERMAN, A. The specialization of the language hemisphere. *Haskins Laboratories Status Report on Speech Research* SR-31/32, 1972.

LIBERMAN, A; COOPER, F.; SHANKWEILER, D.; & STUDDERT-KENNEDY, M. Perception of the speech code. *Psychological Review,* 1967, *74,* 431–461.

LOWE, A., & CAMPBELL, R. Temporal discrimination in aphasoid and normal children. *Journal of Speech and Hearing Research,* 1965, *8,* 313–314.

McKEEVER, W., & HULING, M. Left cerebral hemisphere superiority in tachistoscopic word-recognition and performance. *Perceptual and Motor Skills,* 1970, *30,* 763–766.

McKEEVER, W., & HULING, M. Lateral dominance in tachistoscopic word recognition performances obtained with simultaneous bilateral input. *Neuropsychologia,* 1971, *9,* 15–20.

MILLER, E. Handedness and the pattern of human ability. *British Journal of Psychology,* 1971, *62,* 111–112.

MILNER, B.; BRANCH, C.; & RASMUSSEN, T. Observations on cerebral dominance in R. Oldfield and J. Marshall (Eds.), *Language.* Middlesex: Penguin, 1964.

MOLFESE, D. Cerebral asymmetry in infants, children, and adults; auditory evoked responses to speech and music stimuli. *Journal of the Accoustical Society of America,* 1973, *53,* 363(A).

MORGAN, A.; McDONALD, P.; & MACDONALD, H. Differences in bilateral alpha activity as a function of experimental task, with a note on lateral eye movements and hypnotizability. *Neuropsychologia,* 1971, *9,* 459–469.

NEBES, R. Handedness and the perception of part-whole relationships. *Cortex,* 1971, *7,* 350–356.

NEBES, R., & BRIGGS, C. Handedness and the retention of visual material. *Cortex,* 1974, *10,* 209–214.

NEISSER, U. *Cognitive Psychology* New York: Appleton. 1967.

NEWCOMBE, F., & RATCLIFF, G. Handedness, speech lateralization, and ability. *Neuropsychologia,* 1973, *11,* 399–407.

PAPCUN, G.; KRASHEN, S.; TERBEEK, D.; REMINGTON, R.; & HARSHMAN, R. Is the left hemisphere specialized for speech, language, and/or something else? *Journal of the Acoustical Society of America*, 1974, *55*, 319-327.

POPPEN, R.; STARK, J.; EISONSON, J.; FORREST, T.; & WERTHEIM, G. Visual sequencing performance of asphasic children. *Journal of Speech and Hearing Research*, 1969, *12*, 288-300.

RATCLIFFE, G., & NEWCOMBE, F. Spatial orientation in man: Effects of left, right, and bilateral posterior cerebral lesions. *Journal of Neurology, Neurosurgery, and Psychiatry*, 1973, *36*, 448-454.

RAY, W.; MORELL, M.; FREDIANI, A.; & TUCKER, D. Sex differences and lateral specialization of hemispheric function. *Neuropsychologia*, 1976, *14*, 391-394.

ROBBINS, K., & MCADAM, D. Interhemispheric alpha asymmetry and imagery mode. *Brain and Language* 1974, *2*, 189-193.

ROGERS, L.; TENHOUTEN, W.; KAPLAN, C.; & GARDINER, M. Hemispheric specialization and language: An EEG study of Hopi Indian children. In D. Walter, L. Rogers, & Finzi-Fried (Eds.), *Conference on human brain function 33-40*. Brain Information Service/Brain Research Institute publication BIS, Conference Report #42, UCLA, 1976.

RUSSELL, R., & ESPIR, M. *Traumatic aphasia*. Oxford: Oxford University Press, 1961.

SATZ, P.; ACHENBACH, K.; & FENNELL, E. Correlations between assessed manual laterality and predicted speech laterality in a normal population. *Neuropsychologia*, 1967, *5*, 295-310.

SHANKWEILER, D., & STUDDERT-KENNEDY, M. Identification of consonants and vowels presented to left and right ears. *Quarterly Journal of Experimental Psychology*, 1967, *19*, 59-63.

SPRINGER, S. Ear asymmetry in a dichotic detection task. *Perception and Psychophysics*, 1971, *10*, 239-241.

STUDDERT-KENNEDY, M., & SHANKWEILER, D. Hemispheric specialization for speech perception. *Journal of the Acoustical Society of America*, 1970, *48*, 576-594.

TALLAL, P., & PIERCY, M. Developmental aphasia: Rate of auditory processing and selective impairment of consonant perception. *Neuropsychologia*, 1974, *12*, 83-93.

THOMSON, M. A comparison of laterality effects in dyslexia and controls using verbal dichotic listening. *Neuropsychologia*, 1976, *14*, 243-246.

UMILTA, C.; RIZZOLATTI, G.; MARZI, C; ZAMBONI, G.; FRANZINI, C.; CAMARDA, R.; & BERLUCCHI, G. Hemispheric differences in the discrimination of line orientation. *Neuropsychologia*, 1974, *12*, 165-174.

VAN LANCKER, D., & FROMKIN, V. "Tone" and pitch perception. *Journal of Phonetics*, 1973, *1*, 101-109.

WADA, J.; CLARKE, R.; & HAMM, A. Cerebral hemispheric asymmetry in humans. *Archives of Neurology*, 1975, *32*, 239-246.

WADA, J., & RASMUSSEN, T. Intracarotid injection of sodium amytal for the lateralization of cerebral speech dominance: Experimental and clinical observations. *Journal of Neurosurgery*, 1960, *17*, 266-282.

WARRINGTON, E. AND PRATT, R. Language laterality in left handers assessed by unilateral E.C.T. *Neuropsychologia* 11, 423-428. 1973.

WEISS, M., & HOUSE, A. Perception of dichotically presented vowels. *Journal of the Acoustical Society of America*, 1973, *53*, 51-58.

WEITAN, W., & ETAUGH, C. Lateral eye movements as related to verbal and perceptual-motor skills and values. *Perceptual and Motor Skills*, 1973, *36*, 423-428.

WILLIAMS, M. *Brain Damage and the Mind*. Middlesex: Penguin. 1970.

WITELSON, S., & PALLIE, W. Left hemisphere specialization for language in the newborn. *Brain*, 1973, *96*, 641-646.

WOOD, C.; GOFF, W.; & DAY, R. Auditory evoked potentials during speech perception. *Science*, 1971, *173*, 1248-1251.

ZURIF, E. Auditory lateralization: Prosodic and syntactic factors. *Brain and Language*, 1974, *1*, 391-404.

ZURIF, E., & BRYDEN, M. Familial handedness and left-right differences in auditory and visual perception. *Neuropsychologia*, 1969, *7*, 179-187.

ZURIF, E., & CARSON, G. Dyslexia in relation to cerebral dominance and temporal analysis. *Neuropsychologia*, 1970, *8*, 351-361.

ZURIF, E. & SAIT, P. The role of syntax in dichotic listening. *Neuropsychologia*, 1969, *8*, 239-244.

III

Educational Implications of Recent Research on the Human Brain

7

Some Educational Implications
of Hemispheric Specialization

by Joseph E. Bogen

Dr. Joseph E. Bogen, M.D., is a neurosurgeon who originally performed many of the operations which led to the seminal findings about the hemispheric processes of the brain. For many years a consultant in neurosurgery at the California Institute of Technology, Dr. Bogen is presently senior neurosurgeon of the Ross-Loos Medical Group (Los Angeles) and associate clinical professor of neurosurgery at the University of Southern California School of Medicine. In the following chapter, he discusses the implications of recent brain research for improving education, especially in terms of the brain processes traditionally either emphasized or neglected. He suggests we design education to stimulate development of brain processes in addition to the verbal analytical ones commonly emphasized today in American schools.

It seems that we have finally learned a fact about the brain which bears directly upon everyday pedagogical practice. We now understand that the brain is double, in the sense that each cerebral hemisphere is capable of functioning independently, each in a manner different from the other. Much of the evidence is presented in the preceding chapters, so this chapter is an attempt to summarize and to point out some possible implications of this view of the brain.

One way to look at this new information is to see how it might apply to an ancient problem: the dichotomous nature of *knowing*. I mean by this the conclusion which has been reached by a long series of students of the mind, namely, that we commonly employ two different *kinds of intelligence* or *modes of knowing* or (in a more modern vocabulary) two different *sets of information-processing rules*. After arriving at this conclusion, each scholar has then offered his own favorite dichotomy; Table 7.1 lists some of these. The wide spectrum of thinkers who have arrived at similar conclusions is indicated by the following two examples.

The cognitive psychologist Ulrich Neisser pointed out:

> Historically, psychology has long recognized the existence of two different forms of mental organization. The distinction has been given many names: "rational" vs. "intuitive," constrained" vs. "creative," "logical" vs. "prelogical," "realistic" vs. "autistic," "secondary process" vs. "primary process." To list them together casually may be misleading. . . . nevertheless, a common thread runs through all the dichotomies. (Neisser, 1966, p. 297).

Neisser called one of these *sequential processing;* the other he called *multiple processing*, which carries out many actions simultaneously or at least independently (p. 297).

Sri Aurobindo was a yogic philosopher (handedness apparently unknown) who wrote in 1910:

> The intellect is an organ composed of several groups of functions, divisible into two important classes, the functions and

TABLE 7.1 Terms describing the dichotomous theory of intelligence and the people who used them.

Akhilinanda	buddi	manas
Assagioli	intellect	intuition
Austin	convergent	divergent
Bateson & Jackson	digital	analogic
Blackburn	intellectual	sensuous
Bronowski	deductive	imaginative
Bruner	rational	metaphoric
Cohen	analytic	relational
De Bono	vertical	horizontal
Deikman	active	receptive
Dieudonne	discrete	continuous
Freud	secondary	primary
Goldstein	abstract	concrete
Guilford	convergent	divergent
Hilgard	realistic	impulsive
Hobbes (per Murphy)	directed	free
Humphrey & Zangwill	propositional	imaginative
W. James	differential	existential
A. Jensen	transformational	associative
Kagan & Moss	analytic	relational
D. Lee	lineal	nonlineal
Levi-Strauss	positive	mythic
Levy & Sperry	analytic	gestalt
Lomas & Berkowitz	differentiation	integration
McFie, Piercy (from Spearman)	relations	correlates
McKellar	realistic	autistic
Maslow	rational	intuitive
Neisser	sequential	multiple
Oppenheimer	historical	timeless
Ornstein	analytic	holistic
Pavlov	second signaling	first signaling
C. S. Peirce	explicative	ampliative
Polanyi	explicit	tacit
Price	reductionist	compositionist
Radhakrishnan (per H. Smith)	rational	integral
Reusch	discursive	eidetic
Schenov (per Luria)	successive	simultaneous
Schopenhauer	objective	subjective
C. S. Smith	atomistic	gross
Wells	hierarchical	heterarchical

faculties of the right hand, the functions and faculties of the left. The faculties of the right hand are comprehensive, creative and synthetic; the faculties of the left hand critical and analytic. . . . the left limits itself to ascertained truth, the right grasps that which is still elusive or unascertained. Both are essential to the completeness of the human reason. These important functions of the machine have all to be raised to their highest and finest working-power, if the education of the child is not to be imperfect and onesided. (Aurobindo, 1972; quotation and reference courtesy of Dr. P. Etevenon of Paris.)

One of the difficulties in subscribing to a dichotomous theory of intelligence is that we hardly know which dichotomy to choose because, as Table 7.1 shows, there are so many possibilities. This overabundance of choices is attributable to the ambiguities arising from the *closed-box* approach to the brain.*

In the closed-box approach, one compares input with output and then concludes that the transformations which have occurred require that there be two separate mechanisms or processes within the box whose activity is combined in varying amounts. A given behavioral output can usually be explained in terms of a good many different pairs of hypothesized brain processes. And a choice among the many available pairs is often urged upon us for reasons which are hardly distinguishable from personal idiosyncrasy.

There is a better way: we can open the box and see how it is structured within. What we see, when we do this, is that there are indeed two apparatuses (cerebral hemispheres), each capable of functioning independently in some degree one from the other; and these hemispheres are clearly different in function.

People sometimes ask the question, "Why not three or four

---

*I am aware that this has often been called the "black-box" problem. Although it is appealingly alliterative, continued use of this term reflects, it seems to me, a certain insensitivity to the contemporary social scene.

or more types of intelligence?" A complete answer to this question would involve us in a complicated factor-analytic discussion.*

Possible Characterizations

For now, I would offer a short answer: assuming two types of intelligence, rather than some larger number, not only appeals for reasons of simplicity, but it has the very important advantage of conforming with the physiology of the brain.

A dichotomy which has a sound physiologic basis is one which ascribes the input-output transformations to the interaction of two principle and different types of cognition, each typically identifiable with one of the two cerebral hemispheres. What do we know about these two types of cognition?

The evidence for complementary hemispheric specialization need not be repeated here since it has been extensively reviewed in recent years.† It is now quite clear that one or the other hemisphere will tend to dominate depending upon the nature of the task. Still unsettled, however, is how best to characterize these facts of hemispheric specialization.

One approach is merely to be content with listing the tasks in which each hemisphere predominates. Such a purely descriptive approach leads to many of the same implications for education as does the dichotomous view of intelligence, but it avoids any attempt to condense the abundance of facts into a theoretical model.

In contrast, it is appealing and helpful to suppose that these various tasks have some underlying processes in common—that is,

*Factor analysis is a mathematical method used by some psychologists (and others) to help decide which variables are the most important ones in a multivariate problem.

†See the following references: Benton 1972; Berlucchi 1975; Bogen 1969; Galin 1976; Hécaen 1969; Milner 1971; Nebes 1974; Sperry, Gazzaniga & Bogen 1969; Sperry 1973; Zangwill 1961.

that each hemisphere is specialized for a particular type of information processing which is less available to the other hemisphere. As Liberman (1975) wrote:

> . . . we understand cerebral specialization better when we see all the activities of a hemisphere as reflections of the same underlying design. (P. 43)

What distinguishes one hemisphere from the other is not so much certain specific kinds of material (e.g., words for the left, faces for the right) but the way in which the material is processed. In other words, hemispheric differences are more usefully considered in terms of process specificity rather than material specificity. Levy, Trevarthen, and Sperry (1972) wrote:

> All four of the present tests confirmed in different ways the presence of a fundamental difference in the way the right and left hemispheres perceive things. More than a slight preference in a competitive situation, the results suggest a strong basic differentiation. Where the kind of task being tested could be performed by either left or right hemisphere, the two hemispheres accomplished the same task by characteristically different strategies. (P. 74).

The type of cognition proper to the right hemisphere has been called *appositional,* a usage parallel to the common use by neurologists of *propositional* to encompass the left hemisphere's dominance for speaking, writing, calculation, and related tasks. The word *appositional* is thus an abbreviation for: "according to the rules of information processing which we infer to be typical of the right hemispheres of well-lateralized right-handers."

The study of hemispheric differences is presently occupying a host of investigators; and it would be premature at this time to believe that we know of what appositionality consists. We can, however, say a lot about what it is not; and we have a rapidly accumulating body of evidence indicating what it might be.

First of all, we are *not* here concerned with the difference between thinking and emotion, that is, between intellect and **affect.** Each hemisphere has its own affective apparatus (which is, roughly speaking, its limbic lobe, one in each hemisphere). Furthermore, the affective states of the two hemispheres are usually quite similar. What we are concerned with is how the two hemispheres differ with respect to their *cognitive* capacities.

Much of the earlier work showing a right-hemisphere superiority used the visual sense, so that the right hemisphere appeared to be better at visual or visual-spatial tasks. For example, Zangwill (1961) early on described the hemisphere difference as *propositional versus visuo-spatial.* And a little later we suggested the dichotomy *verbal versus visuo-spatial* (Bogen & Gazzaniga, 1965).

But we now realize that the hemispheres are inadequately distinguished in terms of sensory **modality,** since there is so much evidence for right-hemisphere superiority in certain tasks using the tactile, **kinesthetic,** and auditory modalities. I believe there is some modality specificity, but it is much less important than the process specificity.

To describe appositionality as *spatial* omits its musical and other auditory aspects; and it ignores the obvious need for *spatial perception* in the left-hemisphere act of reading. To characterize appositionality as *synthetic* similarly ignores the synthetic aspects of language formulation, a typically left-hemisphere activity.

Although the left hemisphere is dominant for speaking, reading, calculation, and writing, the right hemisphere is not nonverbal. As pointed out by Gazzaniga in Chapter 4, the right hemispheres of split-brain patients have shown a considerable verbal capacity. We would be in error to consider the right hemisphere less "semantic" than the left. There has even been found some syntactic capability (Zaidel, 1973). But this capability is insufficient, even at best, for the construction of complicated sentences. Propositionality, in other words, is only minimally present in the right hemisphere. We can say, therefore, that the rules of information processing typical of the right hemispheres of well-lateralized right-handers are not the rules characteristic of syntax or linguistic transformation, as discussed in Chapter 6 by Krashen.

What Are the Characteristics of Appositionality?

The right hemisphere is better at the retrieval or recognition of shapes if they are not readily nameable. This suggests that appositionizing excels with stimuli which are sometimes called *configurational.* This term is also useful for describing the greater capability of the right hemisphere for facial recognition as well as certain aspects of musical recognition and production.

It often seems that simultaneous patterns rather than sequential order distinguish appositionality from propositionality. In this connection, it is notable that the block-design test is often done better by the left hands of split-brain patients than by the right. (Bogen & Gazzaniga, 1965). The dominance of the right hemisphere in block-design performance is not an artifact peculiar to operated patients: in normal persons, doing the block-design test more often reduced right-hemisphere alpha waves, in contrast to the usual reduction in left-hemisphere alpha which occurs concurrently with writing. (Galin & Ornstein, 1972). This does not mean that the block-design test is a solely "right-hemisphere test," since the left hemisphere also contributes to the total performance. The proportion of right or left contribution appears to vary with the particular test item, as is probably the case with a variety of other psychological tests.

In Chapter 5 of this book, Nebes reviews evidence showing a

right-hemisphere superiority for *part-whole relationships*, a function also described somewhat synonymously as *gestalt formation* or *closure*. This contrasts with the left-hemisphere predilection for focusing on features or abstracting essentials from a field.

It seemed to me at one time (and still does) that

what may well be the most important distinction between the left and right hemisphere modes is the extent to which a linear *concept* of time participates in the ordering of thought.

In this connection, Harold Gordon and I (Gordon & Bogen, 1974) have recently urged a scheme in which the right hemisphere is specialized for processing time-independent stimulus configurations and the left hemisphere for time-ordered stimulus sequences.

How all of these characterizations can be reconciled, or chosen among, is not yet clear. But without waiting for all the data to arrive, we can summarize to some extent the wealth of information already at hand. Figure 7.1 represents in schematic form such a summary.

In spite of remaining uncertainities, enough is known to motivate some conjectures regarding certain educational policies and practices.

Possible Implications

The notion of two largely lateralized modes of thought suggests that teaching by either lecturing or by imitation affects primarily one or the other hemisphere. Learning of almost any idea is likely to be better if both methods are used. This means that teaching solely by example is as open to the charge of one-sidedness as would be a curriculum consisting solely of lecture courses.

Since education is effective only insofar as it affects the work-

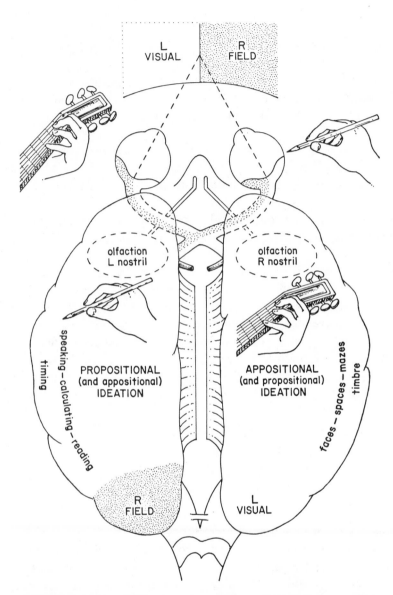

FIGURE 7.1. A schematic outline of the brain as seen from above, to suggest the complementary dominance of the cerebral hemispheres for various tasks, summarizing the evidence from cases of lateralized lesions and from testing of patients with cerebral commissurotomy. Based on version updated and redrawn (by J.E.B.) from the original conception of R.W. Sperry (Sperry, Vogel, and Bogen, 1970).

ing of the brain, we can see that an elementary school program narrowly restricted to reading, writing, and arithmetic will educate mainly one hemisphere, leaving half of an individual's high-level potential unschooled.

We are accustomed to hear, these days, of the *culturally disadvantaged,* a term which often refers to those persons whose propositional potential has remained underdeveloped for lack of relevant exposure. There is likely a parallel lack of appositional development in persons whose only education consists of the "three *R*s." That is, just as the left-hemisphere potential for propositionizing may be underdeveloped, so too should we expect that right-hemisphere capacities can suffer educational neglect.

Has our society tended to overemphasize the values of an analytical attitude, or even of logical reasoning? The physicist Murray Gell-Mann (1970) has stressed the importance of what he calls *preliminary phenomenological schemes* in ordering our observations, beginning with the perception of apparent patterns in the data. Regarding the construction of such schemes, he wrote the following:

> One is guided mainly by the data, . . . sometimes even discarding a few as possibly being experimental errors, . . . and not by deep reasoning from theoretical principles or from underlying dynamical arguments. (P. 3).

The atomic chart of Mendeleev and the evolutionary theory of Darwin were schemes of this sort whose underlying mechanisms were not understood for generations. The overambitious attempt to introduce formal theorizing prematurely can be as unproductive, Gall-Mann says, as either aimless data gathering or the presently fashionable construction of computer models, often on a grandiose scale and often of little relation to the data already available. Gell-Mann concluded:

> Do we sufficiently encourage scheme-makers, particularly qualitative ones? Perhaps in our educational system we lay

too little emphasis on natural history. Perhaps in our schools and universities and throughout the whole battery of intelligence and achievement tests that we use, we do not seek out enough persons with the talent to do the kind of work done by Mendeleev and Darwin. . . . I would like to encourage our society to search for such people, and to support them. (P. 5).

It seems reasonably clear that the difference Gell-Mann has in mind is similar to the one I have already described between propositional and appositional modes of thought. And this dichotomy may help us to understand the difficulties of children who are exceptional in other ways. For example, the extensive experience of Boder (1973) indicates that dyslexics (children with reading problems all out of proportion to their normal intelligence) are of two main types; and it is conceivable that these two main types of dyslexia can result from a maldevelopment of one or the other mode of thought, or perhaps their failure to lateralize in the usual fashion. Related to this are some observations of Geschwind (1972):

One must remember that practically all of us have a significant number of special learning disabilities. . . . For example, I am grossly unmusical and cannot carry a tune. . . . We happen to live in a society in which the child who has trouble learning to read is in difficulty. Yet we have all seen some dyslexic children who draw much better than controls, i.e., who have either superior visual-perception talents, while many of us who function well here might do poorly in a society in which a quite different array of talents was needed to be successful. . . . As the demands of society change, will we acquire a new group of "minimally brain-damaged?" (P. 270)

It is likely that some anatomical asymmetry underlies the potential for hemisphere specialization; but it is also clear that the extent to which capacities are developed is dependent upon environmental exposure. Although humans of any culture, so far as we know, have the potential for reading and writing, many remain nonliterate and thus fall short of acquiring the most special of left-hemisphere functions. Conversely, we can readily comprehend the concept of a society in which "right-hemisphere illiteracy" is the rule. Indeed, our own society (admittedly complex) seems to be, in some respects, a good example: a scholastized, post-Gutenberg-industrialized, computer-happy exaggeration of the Graeco-Roman penchant for propositionizing.

In a recent review of hemispheric specialization, Sperry (1973) wrote:

> The main theme to emerge from the foregoing facts is that there appear to be two modes of thinking, verbal and non-verbal, represented rather separately in left and right hemispheres, respectively, and that our educational system, as well as science in general, tends to neglect the non-verbal form of intellect. What it comes down to is that modern society discriminates against the right hemisphere.

If our society has overemphasized propositionality at the expense of appositionality, more is involved than the adjustment difficulties of a few individuals. It means that the entire student body is being educated lopsidedly. Have not certain pedagogic policies often tended to aggravate and prolong this one-sidedness? For example, the usual justification of IQ tests is that they predict further scholastic achievement and that the latter is in turn predictive of "life success." This is ultimately based upon a criterion of "success" which is not only most often measured monetarily, but seems to depend in part upon an analytic attitude hypertrophied by centuries of contention against nature. It is a view that culminates, when extreme, in measuring national "success" by the gross national product and in measuring progress of the human species in terms of total population. The latter criterion was explicitly adopted by the archeologist V. G. Childe (1951); such a criterion is clear, quantitative, and graphable, but it altogether avoids any concern for the quality of human existence.

It is important to realize that much of our present "intelligence" testing is biased toward abilities more useful in the classroom than in real life. Stanley (1971) did a scholarly review on the prediction of success by the use of the Scholastic Aptitude Tests (SAT). Having meticulously supported with many sources his conclusion that such tests predict success in college, he then resorted to plain old common sense to argue that they also predict "life success." He asked:

> What is the probability that out of 1000 carefully tested eight-year-old boys, who have IQ's of 90, there will emerge even one mathematician or Shakespearean scholar on the Ph.D. level? (P. 645)

Why not a sculptor, singer, painter, poet, or politician? A possible answer to this question is, perhaps, that although a school may enjoy an art or music department, its primary purpose should be to encourage intellectuality, i.e., left-hemisphere potential. Which suggests that many students consider their instruction "irrelevant" not just because they find their courses difficult (as Stanley suggests) but because they view "life success" differently than he does. They are concerned not only with rationality but with sensitivity. They are concerned not so much with making a living as making a life. They see a world of warring elders, busily *becoming* at the expense of *being*, who want them to be unhappy in the same half-brained way. The fight with nature for survival is won, they feel; and it is time we learn to live within nature as bilaterally educated, whole persons.

Such sentiments are difficult to evaluate for various reasons, but that they exist is hardly arguable; and their influence seems to be spreading. We sense about us a growing awareness of the values of the more complex, the interdependent, the nonverbal, and (one is tempted to say) the appositional. The extent to which this is occurring is hardly estimable by me; but I can note a straw in the wind: the use of artwork on the front covers of scientific and medical magazines which for generations were either blank except for the title or consisted of a printed table of contents. For example, the *Journal of the American Medical Association* now routinely uses paintings on its front cover; and the *Journal of Neurosurgery* has used arty covers since 1970.

The search for other-than-left-hemisphere values has not only produced the appearance of art in unfamiliar places, but has also produced a lot of kookiness from sources all too familiar. It is no surprise that if the left hemisphere can produce an impressive variety of chuzzlewit legalisms, jargon, jabberwocky, gobbledygook, and babel, so too can we expect of the right hemisphere its own special and diverse brands of arrant nonsense. There can be what Fischer and Rhead (1974) called

> a rebound effect, characterized by a dramatic overcompen- satory swing toward the cognitive mode of the right hemis- phere to the point of the conspicuous denial of all left hemis- phere values.

Furthermore, hemisphericity (whether preponderantly right or left) varies independently of excellence; the virtue of appositional congruity is probably no easier to acquire than the virtue of pro- positional consistency. So there are some who seem to be barely using either side of their brains.

We can hardly subscribe to the idea that everyone should do his own thing no matter what it is; but there does seem to be a widespread consensus supporting a more eclectic pluralism. It is surely encouraging to find Arthur Jensen (1972), often considered an apostle of less education for certain persons, saying:

> Future solutions will take the form not so much of attempting to minimize differences in scholastic aptitudes and motiva-

tion, but of creating a greater diversity of curricula, instructional methods, and educational goals and values that will make it possible for children ranging over a wider spectrum of abilities and proclivities genuinely to benefit from their years in school. (P. 98)

How shall we proceed to a greater heterogeneity? Can the facts of hemispheric specialization help us avoid the specter of an unbridled diversification including almost any conceivable gimmick, stunt, or deviant viewpoint? One answer might be that we give equal time to each hemisphere. This is not simply a matter of enrichment, but of saving from neglect a cognitive potential as important for high-level problem solving as language skills.

On the one hand, our belief that hemispheric specialization tends to be process-specific rather than material-specific suggests that subject matter my be less important than its method of presentation. Thus, greater right-hemisphere participation would involve more laboratory and field experience at the expense of lectures and seminars. In the teaching of painting, for instance, one could take a relatively more appositional than propositional approach to a subject matter which is itself more appositional than most. Good examples of this are the methods of David Friend (1975), emphasizing the overall "oneness" of a painting or a sketch, rather than the early introduction of drawing or coloring techniques.

On the other hand, subject matter probably *does* make a difference. Although any activity is probably bihemispheric to some degree, the relative hemispheric participation varies considerably. Can we reasonably hope that many hours devoted to the practice of bonsai, ikebana, stitchery, dance, and sculpture will increase the effectiveness of the necessarily decreased time available for courses in physics, forensics, philosophy, and the like? This hope assumes a facilitatory interaction between the two modes of ideation. Such a mutually beneficial reinforcement seems a reasonable expectation, except that there exists some opinion suggesting quite the contrary!

Levy (1972) has hypothesized that the two modes of thought are mutually inhibitory and that their evolutionary lateralization to different hemispheres was to prevent them from interacting detrimentally. Is it possible that the increased savvy of a younger generation raised on TV is causally related to the well-known decline in SAT scores? Mr. Harold Anderson, president of the *Omaha World Herald,* said in an address to the American Newspaper Publishers Association, that the average American high school graduate (as of May 1968) had watched more than 15,000 hours of television as compared with 11,000 hours of formal schooling. The decrease in reading ability may simply result from a lack of training in reading skills. But it may also result in part from an active inhibition of language ability by an intense exposure of the relevant parts of the brain to other activities.

We know that interaction between the two modes of thought is not always detrimental, as is evident from the existence of activities which are typically bihemispheric, symphonic orchestration being an obvious example. But if there are certain circumstances in which mutual inhibition occurs, it would be a matter of high priority for professional educators to learn under which circumstances such a quandary occurs.

It may be a principle virtue of these more recent findings about the brain not only to serve as scientific support for a more diversified curriculum, and not only to provide some direction for this diversification, but also to stimulate a new set of questions for those who will pilot the future of education. We have a few new landmarks; hopefully they will help us to steer a better course.

*   *   *

AUROBINDO, S. The powers of the mind. In *A system of national education.* Pondicherry, India: 1972. Sri Aurobindo Centenary Library.

BENTON, A. L. The "minor" hemisphere. *Journal of the History of Medicine and Allied Sciences,* 1972, *27,* 5–14.

BERLUCCHI, G. Cerebral dominance and interhemispheric communication in normal man. In B. Milner (Ed.), *Hemispheric specialization and interaction.* Cambridge: MIT Press, 1975.

BODER, E. Developmental dyslexia: A diagnostic approach based on three atypical reading-spelling patterns. *Developmental Medicine and Child Neurology,* 1973, *15,* 663–687.

BOGEN, J. E. The other side of the brain, I: Dysgraphia and dyscopia following cerebral commissurotomy. *Bulletin of the Los Angeles Neurological Society,* 1969, *34,* 73–105. (a)

BOGEN, J. E. The other side of the brain, II: An appositional mind. *Bulletin of the Los Angeles Neurological Society,* 1969, *34,* 135–162. (b)

BOGEN, J. E. & BOGEN, G. M. The other side of the brain, III: The corpus callosum and creativity. *Bulletin of the Los Angeles Neurological Society;* 1969, *34,* 191–220.

BOGEN, J. E.; DEZURE, R.; TENHOUTEN, W. D.; & MARSH, J. F. The other side of the brain, IV: The A/P ratio. *Bulletin of the Los Angeles Neurological Society,* 1972, *37,* 49–61.

BOGEN, J. E., & GAZZANIGA, M. S. Cerebral commissurotomy in man: Minor hemisphere dominance for certain visuospatial functions. *Journal of Neurosurgery,* 1965, *23,* 394–399.

CHILDE, V. G. *Man makes himself.* New York: Mentor, 1951.

FISCHER, R., & RHEAD, J. The logical and the intuitive. *Main Currents of Modern Thought,* November/December 1974.

FRIEND, D. *Composition: A painter's guide to basic problems and solutions.* New York: Watson-Guptill, 1975.

GALIN, D. Hemispheric specialization: Implications for psychiatry. In R. G. Grenell & S. Gabay (Eds.), *Biological foundations of psychiatry.* New York: Raven Press, 1976.

GALIN, D., & ORNSTEIN, R. Lateral specialization of cognitive mode: An EEG study. *Psychophysiology,* 1972, *9,* 412–418.

GAZZANIGA, M. S. *The bisected brain.* Englewood Cliffs, N.J.: Prentice-Hall, 1970.

GELL-MANN, M. The value of schemes in scientific theory. in *Proceedings Convegno Mendeleeviano.* Turin: Academy of Science, 1970.

GESCHWIND, N. Disorders of higher cortical function in children. *Clinical Proceedings of the Children's Hospital, National Medical Center,* 1972, *28,* 261-272.

GORDON, H. W., & BOGEN, J. E. Hemispheric lateralization of singing after intracarotid sodium amylobarbitone. *Journal of Neurology, Neurosurgery, and Psychiatry,* 1974, *37,* 727-738.

HÉCAEN, H. Aphasic, apraxic, and agnosic syndromes in right and left hemisphere lesions. *Handbook of Clinical Neurology,* 1969, *4,* 291-311.

JENSEN, A. R. Genetics and education: A second look. *New Scientist,* October 12, 1972, pp. 96-99.

LEVY, J. Lateral specialization of the human brain: Behavioral manifestations and possible evolutionary basis. In J. A. Kiger, (Ed.), *Biology of behavior.* Corvallis: Oregon State University Press, 1972.

LEVY, J.; TREVARTHEN, C.; & SPERRY, R. W. Perception of bilateral chimeric figures following hemispheric deconnexion. *Brain,* 1972, *95,* 61-78.

LIBERMAN, A. M. The specialization of the language hemisphere. In B. Milner (Ed.), *Hemispheric specialization and interaction.* Cambridge: MIT Press, 1975.

MILNER, B. Interhemispheric differences in the localization of psychological processes in man. *British Medical Bulletin,* 1971, *27,* 272-277.

NEBES, R. D. Hemispheric specialization in commissurotomized man. *Psychological Bulletin,* 1974, *81,* 1-14.

NEISSER, U. *Cognitive psychology.* Englewood Cliffs, N.J.: Prentice-Hall, 1966.

SMITH, A. Dominant and nondominant hemispherectomy. in M. Kinsbourne & W. L. Smith (Eds.), *Hemispheric disconnection and cerebral function.* Springfield, Ill.: Thomas, 1974.

SPERRY, R. W. Lateral specialization of cerebral function in the surgically separated hemispheres. in F. J. McGuigan (Ed.), *The psychophysiology of thinking.* New York: Academic Press, 1973.

SPERRY, R. W.; BOGEN, J. E.; & VOGEL, P. J. Syndrome of hemisphere deconnection. In P. Bailey and R. L. Fial (Eds.), *Proceedings of the Second Pan-American Congress of Neurology.* Puerto Rico: Departmente de Instructione, 1970.

SPERRY, R. W.; GAZZANIGA, M. S.; & BOGEN, J. E. Interhemispheric relationships: The neocortical commissures; syndromes of hemisphere disconnection. *Handbook of Clinical Neurology,* 1969, *4,* 273-290.

STANLEY, J. C. Predicting college success of the educationally disadvantaged. *Science,* 1971, *171,* 640-647.

ZAIDEL, E. Linguistic competence and related functions in the right cerebral hemisphere of man following commissurotomy and hemispherectomy. Doctoral thesis, California Institute of Technology, 1973

ZANGWILL, O. L. Asymmetry of cerebral hemisphere function. In H. Garland (Ed.), *Scientific aspects of neurology.* London: Livingstone; 1961.

8

The Generative Processes
of Memory

by M. C. Wittrock

M. C. Wittrock is a professor of educational psychology in the Graduate
School of Education at UCLA specializing in learning and instruction, especially
among children. In the following chapter he traces the history of methods for
stimulating learning and memory from ancient times to current practice. He
shows how central findings from recent research on the processes of the brain
can help explain ways schoolchildren learn. The generative model of learning
he presents emphasizes that verbal processes and imagery can be used to
construct meaning for events and subject matter. He also discusses implications of recent research for teaching and presents the results of an extensive
series of research studies on human learning, reading, and instruction.

Historical Context

To understand some of the meanings and educational implications of the recent research on the human brain, we will begin

with a discussion of the methods developed in ancient Greece and Rome to help teachers, students, orators, and statesmen to remember information, ideas, and speeches. In those days inexpensive writing instruments and books were not readily available to serve as memory aids. In their stead, imagery and mnemonic devices were used to facilitate memory by constructing vivid representations for ideas and information.

ANCIENT TIMES

Simonides, a Greek lyrical poet from Ceos (556–468 B.C.), recorded an ingenious system for teaching people to use imagery to improve their memories.* His system, described in at least three Latin sources (Cicero's *De Oratore,* Quintilian's *Institutio Oratoria,* and the anonymously authored *Rhetorica Ad Herennium*), was taught to many Greek and Roman orators. As established by Isocrates, Greek higher education and later Roman higher education essentially consisted of training in rhetoric, the art of public speaking (Marrou, 1956, pp. 84, 194–205). Without notes or cue cards, orators, statesmen, lawyers, politicians, and teachers spoke in public at great length, sometimes for several consecutive hours. Simonides' system enabled these speakers to remember their many points and arguments in an unambiguous sequence, beginning at any place in the series. The widely taught system was also used to memorize words, quotations, plays, and essays. His system of memory training was centrally important to the classical art of memory, which provides a useful context for understanding recent developments in research in psychology, education, and neurology.

*Frances Yates's excellent book *The Art of Memory* (1966) is the source of many of the facts reported in the historical sections of this paper. However, the quotations presented in this section are all exactly as they appear in the Loeb Classical Library translations. Yates uses some of the same quotations, but she has translated them, altering them slightly. I am deeply indebted to her for her stimulating volume on the art of memory, and to Walter Ong for his several volunes on related issues.

To introduce the classical art of memory excerpts from the three Latin sources summarizing Simonides' system are presented below.

Cicero tersely summarizes Simonides' system, as follows, emphasizing places and images.

> He [Simonides] inferred that persons desiring to train this faculty [memory] must select localities and form mental images of the facts they wish to remember and store those images in the localities, with the result that the arrangement of the localities will preserve the order of the facts, and the images of the facts will designate the facts themselves, and we shall employ the localities and images respectively as a wax writing tablet and letters written on it. (*De Oratore* 2. lxxxvi. 354)

Quintilian, an educator, the foremost teacher of rhetoric in Rome during the first century A.D., taught Simonides' system to orators and students. They were taught to use the rooms and furniture of a familiar building, often their home, as the places or the loci for the images of the events to be remembered (See Figure 8.1)

> The first thought is placed, as it were, in the forecourt; the second, let us say, in the living room; the remainder are placed in due order all around the *impluvium,* and entrusted not merely to bedrooms and parlours, but even to the care of statues and the like. This done, as soon as the memory of the facts requires to be revived, all these places are visited in turn and the various deposits are demanded from their custodians, as the sight of each recalls the respective details (Quintilian, *Institutio Oratoria* 11. 2. 20)

A more detailed description of the memory system is presented in the anonymously authored *Rhetorica Ad Herennium* (3. 17. 30). Part of that description is as follows:

FIGURE 8.1. Photograph courtesy of Alinari-Scala.

We should therefore, if we desire to memorize a large number of items, equip ourselves with a large number of backgrounds, so that in these we may set a large number of images. I likewise think it obligatory to have these backgrounds in a series, so that we may never by confusion in their order be prevented from following the images—proceeding from any background we wish, whatsoever its place in the series, and whether we go forwards or backwards—nor from delivering orally what has been committed to the backgrounds.

The anonymous author later discusses the qualities of images that make them effective for improving memory. His suggestions are highly similar to those given today to learners participating in psychological studies of the effects of imagery upon memory. Ancient and modern directions emphasize distinctive, vivid, active, and comic images constructed by the learner.

> We ought, then, to set up images of a kind that can adhere longest in the memory. And we shall do so if we establish likenesses as striking as possible, if we set up images that are not so many or vague, but doing something; if we assign to them exceptional beauty or singular ugliness, if we dress some of them with crowns or purple cloaks, for example, so that the likeness may be more distinct to us; or if we somehow disfigure them, as by introducing one stained with blood . . . so that its form is more striking, or by assigning certain comic effects to our images, for that too will ensure our remembering them more readily. (*Ad Herennium* 3. 22. 37)

Let us imagine how an orator or student might have been taught to proceed, using Simonides' system. First, the speaker would have had to select a building, order its rooms from first through last, and then order the furniture and other objects within each room in an unambiguous sequence. Beginning with the first object or piece of furniture in the first room, the orator or student would then create and associate active, vivid, dramatic, idiosyncratic, comic, or grotesque images involving his points and his loci. For example, if his first point were to thank the emperor for the privilege of speaking, and his first memory locus was his living room sofa, he might imagine a comically, vividly attired emperor seated on the sofa, actively accepting his thanks. By arranging the loci within a room in a definite order, say clockwise, and then by ordering the rooms in a similar fashion, the orator could establish an unambiguous sequence for remembering his talk.

To comprehend the classical art of memory, we must now turn to Aristotle's theory of memory and recollection, which completes the ancient art of memory as it is known today. The teacher of Alexander the Great and the founder of formal logic believed that imagery was essential to thinking and to remembering. In *De Anima (On the Soul)* and one of its appendices, *On Memory and Recollection*, Aristotle wrote, "It is impossible even to think without a mental picture. The same affection is involved in thinking as in drawing a diagram . . ." (*On Memory and Recollection* 1.450a). Later, in summarizing the section on memory, he writes, "Thus we have explained (a) what memory or remembering is; that it is a state induced by a mental image related as a likeness to that of which it is an image . . ." (*On Memory and Recollection* 1.451b).

In the same paper, Aristotle later presents his two principles of recollection, which were association and order, and his three principles of association, which were similarity, contrast, and contiguity. Aristotle used imagery as the basis of memory, and association and order as the bases for recollection.

Although it was incompatible with Plato's theory of knowledge, Simonides' memory system was supported by Aristotle's writings about imagery in memory, and order and association in recollection. Simonides' memory system and Aristotle's theory of memory and recollection comprised the classical art of memory, which persevered for over a thousand years, until incompatible neoplatonic ideas began gradually to remove it from prominence.

Yates (1966) credits Simonides system for its practical significance to orators and for its important role in convincing Romans that the orators' phenomenal memory was a god-given faculty that defied understanding. In the Roman era, the general populace regarded memory as a divine attribute.

THE MIDDLE AGES

For nearly a thousand years after the many sackings of Rome, only the *Ad Herennium* version of Simonides' memory system survived. During the Dark Ages, oratory probably was not greatly needed nor valued. Rhetoric became largely a temporarily lost art, as did the classical art of memory.

The eleventh and twelfth centuries were the times when scholasticism and religious dogma flourished throughout Europe. With the bloom of religion came the need for effective ways to teach abstract religious ideas to millions of people in Europe. To the scholastics, memory systems again became useful and practical devices for accomplishing their purposes of remembering and making memorable the central Christian ideas which they wished to teach.

Two separate and distinct methods of memory training emerged and flourished during the late medieval period.* The first method was basically a revised version of the classical art of memory of Simonides and Aristotle. Saint Thomas Aquinas and his teacher from Paris, Albertus Magnus, led in the development and spread of the classical art of memory.

Above all others, Thomas Aquinas was responsible for the resurgence of interest in the classical rules for stimulating memory. He wrote that man's mind cannot understand thoughts without images of them, or as he called the images, "phantasmata." In Tomistic thinking, an image is a similitude of a corporeal thing. Saint Thomas believed that the understanding of universals, which to him were the commonalities across particulars (which was Aristotle's concept of them also) necessarily involved imagery. The priests of the Order of Saint Dominic, to which Thomas Aquinas belonged since before he studied with Albert the Great, tolerated and used images only because of what they considered the weakness of man's memory. Images, as physically represented in medieval architecture, painting, and sculpture, were worldly, but still necessary and important as memory aides.

*A third, less influential type of memory system was also found in medieval times (Yates, 1966). The system, which credits Democritus as its originator and Aristotle as the contributor of the laws of association, may have descended through Byzantine cultures. However, the system was not nearly as widespread as the classical and Lullian memory systems. For these two reasons it is not discussed further.

Thomas Aquinas, who was influenced by Aristotle's *De Memoria*, taught and wrote about Aristotle's theory of memory and recollection, including its three laws of association, and the *Ad Herennium* rules for places and images, which are given above. From these classical sources, Aquinas developed four rules for training the memory, which explained how to use images, order, places, and meditation and repetition. His four rules for the training of memory were set forth in a clear, straightforward manner and were widely taught throughout Europe by the Dominican priests. The rules were used by public speakers, especially clergymen, for organizing and remembering speeches and for making abstract religious concepts memorable to their audiences. In medieval times, students were again taught Simonides' art of memory, but now Gothic buildings, their statues and their decorations, were used for the loci and the images.

Frances Yates (1966) suggests that medieval architecture, painting, and sculpture, with their bizarre, grotesque, beautiful, sometimes ugly imagery, were greatly influenced by the rules of the classical art of memory, especially by Thomas Aquinas' writings about them. The bizarre, vivid imagery and personification of abstract verbal ideas (sin, love, hate, heaven, and hell) embodied in the architecture, sculpture, and painting of medieval times may have represented organized memory aids, designed after Simonides' art of memory, to facilitate recall of important religious concepts (Yates, 1966, pp. 95–96). The imagery represented in the gargoyles, statues, figures, and painted glass of medieval buildings may have been a way to elaborate, organize, and make concrete the central abstract religious virtues, vices, rewards, and punishments of the Christian religion. Yates suggests that Dante's *Divine Comedy*, especially the *Inferno*, was a memory system designed to teach people to remember the punishments and rewards that followed their actions by associating them with images of the specific compartments of heaven or hell.

Yates has developed an intriguing hypothesis. To her emphasis on memory aids I would add an emphasis upon the pedagogical value of the imagery represented in medieval statues, paintings, and buildings. Together these two emphases suggest that modern scholars may have misunderstood the psychology and character of many medieval people by generalizing about them from the grotesque and fanciful figures which adorned their buildings and paintings. Perhaps, without ready access to inexpensive teaching aids such as printed pages, some of the spiritual and intellectual leaders of medieval societies adopted and used the classical art of memory to design paintings, buildings, and statues to help them teach the central ideas of the Christian religion. If Yates's hypothesis is sound, it is ironic that the pagan concept of using images to facilitate memory should have survived through medieval times because it was an effective tool for teaching Christian dogma, vices, and virtues.

In sharp contrast to the memory-training system of Thomas Aquinas, which was basically a revival and recombination of the rules of memory of Aristotle and the *Ad Herennium* version of Simonides' system, was a system developed by Ramon Lull, the second major memory system widely used during the Renaissance. Born ten years after Thomas Aquinas, Lull devoted much of his adult life to the development of his abstract verbal system for training the memory.

Lull, an eccentric whose thinking was far removed from medieval philosophy, used almost no dramatic images or corporeal similitudes in his memory system. Instead he used letters, divine attributes, abstract symbols, abstract ideas, and dynamic loci which revolved on concentric circles called memory wheels (e.g., *Ars Magna*, pp. 1–4). His system was designed to help one remember all subject matters.

In his system were the attributes of Goodness, Greatness, Eternity, Power, Wisdom, Will, Virtue, Truth, and Glory. Each of these nine attributes was used at each of the following levels leading into the house of wisdom. In descending order, the levels were (1) God, (2) angels, (3) stars, (4) man, (5) imagination, (6) animals, (7) plants, (8) elements, and (9) the virtues and the arts and sciences. The configuration of nine attributes at each of nine levels yielded 81 loci useful for remembering information in an organized way.

Lull also used other, more pictorial representations (*Le Livre Des Bêtes,* pp. 48, 64, 80, 96, et passim), including one where the branches and roots of a tree comprise an encyclopedic system of knowledge (*Arbor Scientiae*). In all of Lull's visual representations of verbal knowledge there are few vivid images as taught by the originators of the classical memory system. Instead, in Lullian diagrams we usually find abstract formulas, verbal symbols, words, names, and attributes.

The Lullian system seems more compatible with neoplatonic ideas than with scholasticism and the Aristotelian laws of association and reminiscence, with Renaissance ideas more than with medieval philosophy and psychology. Even so, the Lullian system still represents a visual, spatial organization of verbal concepts.

As the Dominican friars taught and circulated Thomas Aquinas' revival of the classical art of memory, the Franciscan fathers learned and circulated the Lullian memory system.

In the sixteenth century, a chair of Lullism was established at the Sorbonne. The first holder of the chair, Bernardus de Lavinheta, recommended and taught the classical memory system of Simonides and Aquinas for remembering "sensibilia," and the Lullian system for remembering "initelligiblia." Lavinheta's synthesis represented the two major memory systems that dominated the medieval era.

THE RENAISSANCE

During the Renaissance, sweeping changes occurred in psychology, in philosophy, and in the spirit of the times. These changes were reflected in education, in teaching, and in the training of memory.

In ancient times, imagination was used to compose striking images to aid people, especially orators, to learn and to remember their speeches. In the Middle Ages, the earthly and base imagination was used to compensate for what was considered the human weakness in memory. Images became euphemistically termed "corporeal similitudes," which were needed to aid the weak mental faculty of memory.

Among the changes in psychology during the Renaissance was a new concept of cognition, especially imagination. Imagination rose from its earthly, venal, medieval status to become a divine and magically powerful faculty. In the Renaissance imagination became the essence of the art of facilitating learning and memory, which then became a constructive process of generating new secular knowledge as well as the more familiar process of remembering previously learned religious concepts. In the Renaissance it was believed that through his divine and magical imagination, man could understand the entire universe, especially with the aid of organized, magical memory systems. The new self-confidence in man's imagination must surely have been an important factor in producing a rebirth of learning, invention, and discovery.

Among the changes in philosophy of the Renaissance was the neoplatonic conception of the primacy of abstract ideas. This conception intruded upon the Aristotelian concept of ideas or universals being the commonalities across the particulars. Platonic conceptions of knowledge and ideas deemphasized the role of imagery in learning and in understanding.

The above changes in philosophy and psychology are represented in the changes in ways people during the Renaissance learned to remember organized bodies of information and subject matter. In addition, the increasing technological sophistication of the times influenced the training of memory. The printed book became an effective memory aid which greatly affected the memory systems that teachers and preachers used to remember their ideas and to make them memorable to their charges.

The two distinct, highly prominent memory systems of medieval times—the classical system, as revived by Thomas

Aquinas and circulated by the Dominicans, and the Lullian system, invented by Ramon Lull and taught by the Franciscan fathers — led to complicated, highly elaborate memory systems during the Renaissance. The complicated Renaissance systems based upon using the imagination were used as magical ways to generate new knowledge.

Guilio Camillo's memory theater (Yates, 1966) is an excellent representation of such Renaissance memory systems. Camillo's wooden theater was crowded with images. However, the places and the images were strictly Renaissance, not medieval, in character. The theater was hierarchically organized into seven levels divided into seven gangways. The seven gangways represented the seven planets; and each of the seven levels represented a dimension of knowledge, with the lowest layer representing the most fundamental.

The seven planets and their images represented the first layer of knowledge and also provided the names for the seven gangways. The second layer of knowledge was represented by images of a banquet given to the gods, which symbolized the first day of creation in Homeric mythology. The third level depicted a cave, which in the *Odyssey* symbolized a further stage in man's creation. The other levels represented the creation of man's soul, soul and body, man's behavior, culture, art, science, and so on. These two series then represented the two dimensions of an organized system of the knowledge of the universe. For example, in the banquet level, the image for the planet Jupiter represented air as a simple element, while the same image appearing in the next higher layer, the cave, represented air as a mixed element (Paivio, 1971, p. 164). In Camillo's theater we find the classical rules for images and places adapted to a Renaissance, magical, ambitious representation of the organization of all knowledge of the world.

Giordano Bruno, a Dominican born in 1548, devoted his life to philosophy and to the construction of memory systems. Many volumes have been written about this extraordinary man, including one by Frances Yates (*Giordano Bruno and the Hermetic Tra-*

dition, 1964). Bruno combined the classical memory system with Lullian ideas. Bruno meshed Thomas Aquinas' four rules for memory with images from the zodiac, astrology, and the planets. As in Lull's system, Bruno placed these magical images on revolving concentric circles; each with thirty segments. In his most complicated system he combined the round Lullian system with a square system composed of memory rooms, each divided into nine memory places, which were further divided into representations of the physical world, man's culture, and knowledge. Bruno seems to have combined in his systems nearly every principle we have previously encountered.

Camillo's and Bruno's systems represented a revolution in the Renaissance in thinking and in attitude about imagination. From the lowly status of a base faculty, imagination had acquired magical properties and had risen to a divine status, where ironically memory had been since ancient days.

The memory systems of the Renaissance reflected a related change in the training of memory. Although the systems still used visual and spatial configurations, the Renaissance memory systems were becoming increasingly abstract and verbal and were used for generating new knowledge. Words, not striking images, appeared commonly in them. The physical universe and the discovery of knowledge about it became the central concern. The religious vices and virtues remained in the systems, but they became part of a larger whole.

Perhaps printed words and books, perhaps also the discoveries of scientists, were producing these effects upon the art of memory. In any event, new ways were needed in the Renaissance to organize, to communicate, and to remember the burst of knowledge about the physical universe and to express the new confident conception of man's creative intellectual powers. The tried and venerable classical memory-training techniques were modified to accommodate the problems of the times and the emphasis on verbal symbols and universals. However, the techniques became more generative and hierarchical, with the printed words and abstract symbols appearing contiguously with the concrete images representing them.

The best example of the continuation of the progression of events described above was the memory system of a sixteenth-century reformer of educational methods, Pierre de La Ramée (Peter Ramus), a French dialectician (1515-1572). His master's examination thesis was rashly entitled "All That Aristotle Has Said Is False" (Graves, 1912, p. 26). He introduced a "dialectical order" that nearly abolished the classical art of memory. W. S. Ong also discusses Ramus's contribution in *Ramus: Method and the Decay of Dialogue* (1958) and another book (Ong, 1971).

In place of images, Ramus substituted hierarchical arrays of words in which, as in an organizational chart, the most general categories are given first. These categories are divided into sub-parts or sub-categories, which in turn are further subdivided. Gone were the images and places and the classical rules for them. Spatial organization and visualization of hierarchical relations were still present. But the representation was more abstract and verbal, without the imaginative figures and the concrete images common to most ancient, medieval, and Renaissance memory systems.

It is interesting to note that in his forties, Ramus became a Protestant convert, openly critical of the imagery in Catholic churches and in Greek and Roman architecture. With his disdain for imagery, Ramus reformed teaching methods in France. His dialectical order, with its focus upon hierarchical organization, introduced a new emphasis on abstract but hierarchical verbal relationships in school learning.

MODERN TIMES

Memory systems declined in influence after the Renaissance, although they were still known and used by some scholars. Francis Bacon wrote about memory systems and images, as did Descartes.

Leibnitz apparently knew the memory treatises well and was influenced by Lull's system. Nonetheless, the standard images used in the organized memory systems declined within men's minds as quickly as did their external counterparts, the statues and the ornaments that formerly graced their buildings.

In modern times variations of the above systems appeared, with the loci adapted to the changing interests and problems of the learners. For example, in England in the seventeenth century, Robert Fludd, a medical doctor, developed a square system using a theater resembling the Globe theater, and a round system using celestial images.

However, the memory systems, especially their generative characteristics, were rapidly declining and falling into disrepute, becoming used primarily as **mnemonics** (memory aids). For example, Gregor von Feinagle* used rooms with images associated with numbered areas on the walls, floors, and ceilings. To remember numbers, dates, and historical events, the numbers were coded into words, using consonants to represent the ordered digits. An image in the room was used to represent the event. One part of the image was the word whose consonants could be decoded into the year of the historical event. Related mnemonic systems based upon imagery still exist today, but they are no longer in the mainstream of educational methods.

The causes of the decline and fall of the use of imagery in training memory in post-Renaissance times are not well understood. Perhaps this decline was due to the new availability of inexpensive writing instruments and printed books, and, if you are a daring speculator, perhaps to an increasing dominance of the left hemisphere over the right hemisphere. The Neoplatonic movement in philosophy and the Protestant Reformation, which disparaged the use of imagery in the sculpture, painting, and

---

Webster's New Word Dictionary, College Edition (1964) states that the word *finagle* (or *fenagle* is a "probable respelling of Fenaigle, G." and means "to cheat, get by trickery, or, in card games, to renege or revoke." However, the word may derive its meaning from Fenaigle's expertise in whist.

architecture of ancient, medieval, and Renaissance cultures, may also have diminished the need to use imagery to facilitate learning and memory in schools. (See Yates, 1966 for further discussion of the training of memory.)

Whatever the reasons for the decline and fall after the Renaissance of the use of imagery to facilitate learning and memory, an understanding of the history of the art of training the memory provides an excellent context for understanding recent research in cognition, educational methods, and the lateralization of processes of the human brain. Since about 1950 there has been a renewal of interest in the use of imagery to facilitate memory and understanding*

Recent Research

The new shift in emphasis, I believe is the result of the decline of one line of research, the rise of several relatively independent but converging lines of research, the ubiquitousness of television and movies, and a new belief in the dignity of the individual in a technological society. First, there is the recent decline of behaviorism which prevailed in America from 1900 to about 1950 in research in psychology, in educational psychology, and in education.† In this area, the positivism of American behaviorists directed

---

*Walter Ong (1971) interprets the progression differently. He views the progression as a continual increase in the visual presentation of information through and including contemporary American society. See also his other works on the same theme (1958, 1967, 1968).

†The heavy American emphasis on functional behaviorism may have helped to bring about the fall of interest in imagery in psychology. Paivio (1971, p. 167) states, "Behaviorism in general represented a "protestant reformation" movement in psychology, and Watson's rejection of imagery and his concomitant emphasis on verbal processes as the mechanism of thought (including memory) in particular bears a striking resemblance to Perkins' earlier rejection of Brunian memory and his advocation of Ramism."

research away from cognitive processes, such as thinking, attention, memory, and imagery. Educational psychology was part of the trend, to the point of disparaging cognitive conceptualizations of school learning.

Within that behavioristic theory, school learning and teaching were often conceived as the art of getting students to practice verbal or motor behavior to obtain reinforcement or reward. That is, school learning was often conceived primarily as the operant or instrumental conditioning of stimuli to responses.

Within the last several years, the dominant paradigm for research in education is beginning to shift as a result of the findings from several lines of research. Ironically, even the research on computer technology has helped to lead researchers to hypothesize internal cognitive processing devices, such as buffers, memory, and storage.

At a popular level, television and movies brought active, dramatic, bizarre, and comical images into the daily lives of most Americans. The impact of these media has been written about frequently elsewhere, although not in terms of their mnemonic and generative characteristics as I am suggesting here. Nonetheless, I will not elaborate upon the deep effects of the media upon our values and lives.

In psychology, the shift to research on memory and away from immediate performance hastened the reconstruction of internal cognitive states to mediate across the time between learning and delayed performance. Also in psychology, interest in modeling and observational learning led to the reconsideration of the values of positing hypothetical cognitive states, such as attention, motivation, and imagery, to explain how learning is retained and retrieved.

Almost simultaneously with the these renewed interests in memory, computer technology, and observational learning came the independently discovered findings of the researchers studying the lateralization of the human brain. Their findings, some of which are reported in other chapters, have fundamental significance for understanding human learning and memory, for integrating the several lines of research mentioned above, and for advancing knowledge about teaching and instruction.

The historical context that I developed above will aid in the understanding of recent findings and recent theories and models. The earliest of the research reported below, done by my students and me, was conducted independently of the recent brain research. However, our data are quite compatible with the findings of this research, which supply us new explanations and hypotheses. Our interests now center upon converging these lines of research into a model of the generative processes of learning and remembering, and upon understanding and facilitating the processing systems of the brain. Below are some of the findings of our research and related research by other people.

IMAGERY AND SPATIAL ELABORATION

Allan Paivio (1971) describes empirical studies on imagery. Most of these studies indicate that the following three imaginal techniques facilitate recall in psychological laboratories.

First, instructions to the learner to "image" the information to be remembered usually facilitates recall. If the learner develops an interactive image involving two or more of the words to be remembered, recall is facilitated. Second, high-imagery words (i. e., concrete words) usually produce a sizable facilitation of recall. Third, pictures facilitate recall of the objects or concepts they represent. Paivio writes that imagery is the single most important variable determining free recall in his studies (1971).

Studies with schoolchildren also usually indicate that instructions, pictures, and high-imagery words facilitate learning and recall, although the size of the effect is often less than that obtained in the laboratory. At UCLA several experiments were conducted to determine if kinetic molecular theory could be taught to kindergarteners and primary school children using pictures, concrete examples, and simple verbal text to introduce and explain the concepts of molecules in motion, states of matter, and changes in states of matter (Keislar & McNeil, 1962; Wittrock, 1963). Several hundred original colored drawings prepared by artists were used to represent molecules, gases, liquids, solids, evaporation, and condensation. After two to four weeks of instruction, two-thirds of the children in one study (Wittrock, 1963) successfully learned and remembered the concepts one year later. These concepts were previously thought to be too complicated for children below Piaget's symbolic (age eleven) or concrete (age seven) levels of intellectual development.

But in this study the verbal abstractions were all iconically presented, using concrete examples familiar to the child. The verbal and the spatial materials were presented simultaneously, perhaps allowing the two to interact, and perhaps allowing the spatial materials to elaborate and make more specific the abstract verbal concepts.

In another study (Wittrock, 1967), primary school children were taught to solve problems using cards with pictures pasted on them to represent the four hypotheses they were to test. These concrete pictorial representations of abstract hypotheses enabled the children to outperform the control group given the same instruction and problems but no cards. A third group given the cards plus a procedure for testing each hypothesis in turn — by "hanging the hypothesis card on a hook and discarding the card after refuting the hypothesis" — performed the best of the three groups, even on transfer tests where the problems and hypotheses were new and the cards were unavailable.

In a more recent study (Bull & Wittrock, 1973) definitions of vocabulary words were taught to elementary school children. We compared three different procedures:

- Read and write the words and their definitions (verbal).
- Read the definition and trace the picture of it (image given).

- Read the definition and draw your own picture to represent the definition (generate an image).

We predicted and found that generating images would produce the best recall, tracing images the second best recall, and learning the words only, the lowest recall. These differences were statistically significant but not large.

We explained the results as follows. Learning verbal materials by elaborating them imaginally enhances their recall probably because they are processed in two interacting ways. Compared with tracing, generating one's own image of each word further increases recall probably because it stimulates relating the new abstract term to one's experience, giving it a distinctive meaning

VERBAL AND SEMANTIC PROCESSING

The findings of laboratory experiments in psychology, in which verbal organizations are constructed by learners, sometimes include sizable effects upon memory. Bower and Clark (1969) gave college students twelve tests of ten unrelated nouns. The control group was asked to learn and to remember the ordered lists in whatever way they wished. The experimental group was asked to make a story from the words of each list. The control group remembered 14 percent of the ordered lists of words. The experimental group remembered 93 percent of them. With results as impressive as these, statistical tests seem superfluous.

In another study, Bower, Clark, Lesgold, and Winzenz (1969) used three different hierarchical arrays of words: (1) unrelated words, (2) randomly arrayed conceptually related words, and (3) properly arrayed conceptually related words. Recall of the words increased with the increases in their verbal and spatial organization from group 1 through group 3.

In a related study (Wittrock & Carter, 1975) the same three treatments were presented, but with instructions either to process the words *generatively* (rearrange them until they fitted a logical pattern) or to process them reproductively (copy them). The results found by Bower et al. were replicated in the copying treatment. More importantly, the **generative processing** condition greatly increased retention in each condition, usually doubling it, even when there was no logical pattern to be discovered.

This study suggests that in addition to the type of representation, verbal or imaginal, the kind of processing performed by the learner is important. When the learner relates new information to his experience and is required to construct associations or meaning involving the new information, his learning and recall is facilitated. The above study provided a useful test of the *generative hypothesis,* which I have been developing over a number of years. Unlike semantic processing hypotheses, which suggest that meaningful learning is primarily a process of constructing abstract verbal associations or dictionarylike lexical meanings, the generative hypothesis interprets learning primarily as the construction of concrete, specific verbal and imaginal associations, using one's prior experience as part of context for the construction. It is a model of learning as the transfer of previous learning.

The generative hypothesis has been investigated in several experiments on reading (Marks, Doctorow, and Wittrock, 1974; Wittrock, Doctorow, and Marks, 1975; and Doctorow, Wittrock, and Marks, in preparation), the latest one of which will be briefly described in Figure 8.2. In it, children read commercially published stories commonly used in public schools to teach reading. As they read these stories, the children were asked to generate (G) headings for each paragraph of each story, or were given one (O_1) or two-word (O_2) organizers for each paragraph, or were asked to read stories in the three control groups (C). From the generative hypothesis I predicted the experimental treatments to rank above the control treatments, and from high to low in the left-to-

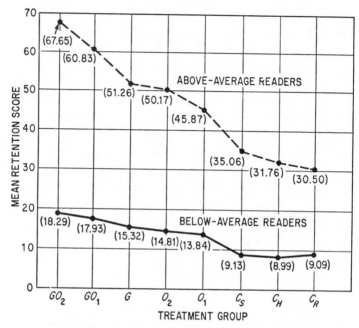

FIGURE 8.2. Mean retention scores for above-average and below-average readers. (Adapted from an article by the author appearing in the 1974 *Educational Psychologist,* 11, *2,* 89. Copyrighted by the American Psychological Association, Inc., 1974).

right order indicated in Figure 8.2. As the figure indicates the predicted rank order occurs without exception in both experiments with the measures of comprehension and recall ($p < .001$).

In sum, it appears that when schoolchildren process information generatively their learning and recall is facilitated, sometimes dramatically. These results are quite compatible with research on the human brain, which helps us understand why and how what we have called verbal and imaginal processing techniques may produce their effects in the classroom and in the laboratory.

For the future, we need to study and learn more about how our teaching techniques can be designed to stimulate the two hemispheres and their processes to interact with one another to construct representations that are long remembered. That is, having analyzed some of the different processes of the brain, we now need to synthesize them into an understanding of how they relate to each other in complicated educational contexts, such as the teaching of reading, mathematics, art, and music. We also need to determine when an interaction between brain processes is inhibitory to learning.

RELATED THEORETICAL MODELS
AND EDUCATIONAL RESEARCH

There are additional theoretical and empirical lines of research that are investigating closely related problems, a few of which are briefly mentioned below.

First of all, a large number of studies have been conducted on the effects produced by inserting into texts a number of adjunct questions for the readers to answer. These complicated findings are well summarized in a chapter by Anderson and Biddle (1975). As they indicate, the recent research on adjunct questions has involved little theorizing. Unfortunately, the interesting data have not been adequately synthesized into a model nor closely related to cognitively oriented research and research on human brain processes.

In his *dual-processing model* of encoding, Allan Paivio (1971) has related much of the recent laboratory research on imagery and verbal processing of information to the recent research on the human brain. He posits two separate but interacting systems of encoding and storing information: *verbal processing* and *imaginal processing*. He cites a wealth of research data to support his model.

However, in one area of research—the study of the effects of instructions to process words either verbally or imaginally—the data often conflict with Paivio's model. To try to reconcile these conflicting findings, two recent experiments were conducted (Wittrock & Goldberg, 1975) in which verbal processing and imaginal processing were varied in the instructions to the learners and in the characteristics of the words to be remembered. We hypothesized that the studies conflicting with the dual-processing model may not have considered the strong imaginal or verbal associations of the words to be learned. These characteristics, developed over many years, may be more important than the instructions.

In our studies, one with college learners and one with junior high school learners, the conflict was resolved. More specifically, high-imagery words tended to be imaginally processed regardless of the instructions to process them verbally. The reverse was true for words high in verbal meaningfulness but low in imagery. After reexamining the findings of other studies in terms of word associations rather than instructions, we discovered that most of the findings ostensibly disagreeing with a dual-process theory are actually consistent with it. Word meanings have developed over many years. As a result, they tend to override the situational effects of directions, at least when the directions involve a type of processing contrary to the learner's long history of experience with the words.

School Learning as a Generative Process

In the context of the historical events mentioned above and of the recent research on the human brain, imagery, and semantic and verbal processing, I suggest that learning in schools be reconceived as a generative cognitive process (see Wittrock, 1974). That is, learning involves the active construction of meaning for stimuli, using verbal processing, imaginal processing (or propositional and appositional processing), and perhaps other types of processing. From this point of view, it is plausible that learning is basically a process of relating stimuli to previous experience, from which one induces and elaborates meanings and representations. According to this model, learning with understanding is the process of transferring previous experience to new events and problems. This position is quite compatible with recent brain research and with the classical art of training the memory.

In this view, teaching is more than the reinforcement of correct responses in the presence of discriminative stimuli. In large part teaching is the process of organizing and relating new information to the learner's previous experience, stimulating him to construct his own representations for what he is encountering. Students learn by active construction of meaning, by what reactions the teacher causes them to generate.

Implications for Teaching

The recent research on the brain has implications for fundamental changes in education. In Chapter 7, J. E. Bogen has cogently discussed many of these important implications, including educating both hemispheres, the need to increase diversity in curricula and methods, and the newly found basis for reemphasizing methods of learning. In the following paragraphs, I would like to emphasize three educational implications from the research presented in this and preceding chapters.

First, the research presented in this book indicates the importance of understanding that people process information in different and multiple ways which may interact with one another. We have also found that we can facilitate learning by stimulating generative processing of information. The first implication of these findings is that the art of teaching needs to devise sophisticated ways to facilitate the multiple processing systems of the brain.

Second, the research described in this book gives us some new insights into old issues, such as the teaching of reading and inductive-deductive learning. In the case of reading, a complex set of cognitive processes is involved, as the brain hemispheres work in conjunction with each other in recognizing shapes and **phonemes,** in associating meanings with syllables and words, in comprehending sentence and story meaning by relating previous learning to the text, and in converting meaning into speech, including selecting syllables, intonation, pitch, and stress. Reading then is a much more complicated process than some of us thought it was.

The recent research mentioned above also gives us a better understanding of a wide range of reading problems, such as dyslexia, developmental lag, and incomplete cerebral dominance. For example, suppose that, as Gazzaniga (1970) summarizes it, very young children have language present in both hemispheres and have an incompletely developed corpus callosum. Through growth and developmental processes and through stimulation from people and experience, the left hemisphere gradually becomes dominant for sequential, verbal-semantic, or propositional functions, the right hemisphere for simultaneous, spatial-imaginal, appositional functions, and the corpus callosum matures and interconnects the two more completely. If any of these growth or developmental processes do not occur properly, a reading problem will appear.

Even if these processes occur normally, stimulation of the processes of the brain in interaction with each other would still be important in facilitating the learning of language and reading, as has been found in several empirical studies. Moeser and Bregman (1973) successfully used pictures to improve the teaching of syntax. Yarmey and Bower (1972) used imagery instructions to raise the performance of educable retarded children to the level of normal children on **paired-associate tasks.** Levin (1973) found that both good and poor readers improved their comprehension after imagery instructions. Children with vocabularies more than one year below grade level were helped most with the pictures.

Although it is only a beginning at understanding the complexities of reading, the above conception suggests one interesting analysis of the facilitation of reading: Children may need practice at associating the sounds and semantic meanings of words, primarily on the left side, with the recognition of their shapes, primarily on the right side.

In addition, the research summarized in this book should help us to develop new diagnostic tests of sequential verbal-auditory processes and of simultaneous visual-spatial ones and, perhaps someday, measures of their connectedness. The recent research should elucidate the need to tailor reading methods to the aptitudes or disabilities of the learners. The long quest for a universally superior reading method, one that was to be better for nearly all students, may have been a futile one. It now seems more advantageous to study methods in relation to aptitudes and to the processes used by the brain to construct meanings and representations for printed words.

For my third implication, let us discuss recent research which may suggest new concepts about methods of presenting subject matter. As Krashen mentioned in Chapter 6, one of the graduate students at UCLA, Dayle Hartnett (1974), hypothesized and found an interaction between brain hemispheric dominance and effectiveness of inductive and deductive methods of teaching Spanish. Inductive learning, which involved synthesizing parts into wholes was presented in the curriculum prepared by Dr. J. Barcia. Inductive learning was as effective or more effective than deductive learning for right-hemisphere-dominant students. Deductive learning, which proceeds from the rules to the examples, was more effective for left-hemisphere-dominant learners studying the curriculum prepared by Dr. W. Bull. This interesting study indicates a way to theorize about how instructional treatments may interact with aptitudes or with brain processes.

In matching teaching methods to aptitudes or processes, there is the issue of which mode should be the dominant or primary mode of instruction and which mode should be the elaborative mode. Instruction may often be better when multiple modes are used, not just the learner's dominant mode. One important educational issue seems to be, not the determination of a single mode for a learner, but rather the selection of which primary mode is to be excited simultaneously with which secondary one to stimulate an interaction between the hemispheres.

The issue is complicated by the realization that in the design of instruction the nominal stimuli — for example, pictures — must be understood in terms of the type of processing, verbal-semantic or imaginal, they stimulate among learners. Although pictures are normally processed imaginally, an instructional method using pictures might stimulate the learners to describe these pictures with sentences. In that sense, what appears to be a pictorial method of instruction might better be understood as a verbal-semantic one, or perhaps an interactive one, involving imagery and semantic-verbal processes. The mode of instruction may not be important. The important point is that the treatment must be understood in terms of the types of processing of information it stimulates, not only in terms of its nominal characteristics.

Summary

The theme of this chapter is that learning and memory are generative processes. The major educational implication of the theme is that the methods of teaching should be designed to stimulate students actively to construct meaning from their experience, rather than stimulating them to reproduce the knowledge of others without relating that knowledge to their own experience.

From ancient times through modern days the theme of learning and memory as constructive processes recurs. Simonides viewed remembering as a constructive process. By having students use their previous experience to construct imaginal representations for verbal concepts, he taught them how to improve their memories. His ingenious procedure, in itself not important today, becomes significant when it is related to the subsequent events of the Middle Ages and the Renaissance and to current research findings. In these contexts, I suggest that we may not fully appreciate the pedagogical and mnemonic value of imagery concretely represented in architecture, painting, and sculpture.

The findings of the recent research on the lateralization processes of the human brain provide scientific evidence which indicates that learning and memory are processes that often involve constructing representations in both brain hemispheres. Zaidel and Sperry (1974, p. 270) summarize their related findings as follows:

> Taken collectively, the results support the conclusion that the inter-hemispheric commissures are important to memory especially in the initial grasping and sorting-for-storage of perceived information, and at later stages in the retrieval and read-out of contralateral or bilateral engrams.

Later, on the same page, they conclude their article as follows:

> In particular the data suggest that processes mediating the initial encoding of engrams and the retrieval and read-out of contralateral engram elements involve hemispheric co-operation and depend upon the functions of the inter-hemispheric commisures.

In one sense we are where we started with this chapter, with Simonides and his discovery of the facilitating effect upon memory of constructing imaginal representations for words and sentences. In another sense, we are far ahead of Simonides. The findings of recent research from several lines of inquiry indicate that we can facilitate learning with understanding and comprehension by stimulating the brain to process information generatively.

* * *

ANDERSON, R. C., & BIDDLE, W. B. On asking people questions about what they are reading. In G. Bower (Ed.), *Psychology of learning and motivation* (Vol. 9). New York: Academic Press, 1975.

Anonymous. *Rhetorica ad herennium* (trans. Henry Caplan). Cambridge: Harvard University Press, Loeb Classical Library, 1967.

ARISTOTLE. *On the soul (De Anima); Parva naturalia; and On breath* (trans. W. H. Hett). Cambridge: Harvard University Press, Loeb Classical Library, 1964.

BOWER, G. H., & CLARK, M. C. Narrative stories as mediators for serial learning. *Psychonomic Science,* 1969, *14,* 181–182.

BOWER, G. H.; CLARK, M. C.; LESGOLD, A. M.; : WINZENZ, D. Hierarchical retrieval schemes in recall of categorized word lists. *Journal of Verbal Learning and Verbal Behavior,* 1969, *8,* 323–343.

BULL, B. L., & WITTROCK, M. C. Imagery in the learning of verbal definitions. *British Journal of Educational Psychology,* 1973, *43,* 289–293.

CICERO. *De oratore* (trans. E. W. Sutton). Cambridge: Harvard University Press, Loeb Classical Library, 1967.

DANTE ALIGHIERI. *The Inferno* (trans. John Ciardi). New Brunswick, N.J.: Rutgers University Press, 1954.

DOCTOROW, M.; WITTROCK, M. C.; & MARKS, C. Generative processes in reading comprehension. *Journal of Educational Psychology,* in Press.

GAZZANIGA, M. S. *The bisected brain.* New York: Appleton-Century-Crofts, 1970.

GRAVES, F. P. *Peter Ramus and the educational reformation of the sixteenth century.* New York: Macmillan, 1912.

HARTNETT, D. The relation of cognitive style and hemisphere preference to deductive and inductive second language learning. Paper read at UCLA Conference on Human Brain Function, Los Angeles, September 27, 1974.

KEISLAR, E., & McNEIL, J. Teaching science and mathematics by auto-instruction in the primary grades: An experimental strategy in curriculum development. In J. F. Coulson (Ed.), *Programmed learning and computer-based instruction.* New York: Wiley, 1962.

LEVIN, J. R. Inducing comprehension in poor readers: A test of a recent model. *Journal of Educational Psychology,* 1973, *65,* 19–24.

LULL, R. *Arbor scientiae.* Lyons, France, 1515.

LULL, R. *Ars magna generales et ultima.* Lyons, France: Maréchal, 1517.

LULL, R. *Le livre des bêtes.* (translation into French by Armand Llinanes). Paris: Librairie C. Klincksieck, 1964.

MARKS, C. B.; DOCTOROW, M. J.; & WITTROCK, M. C. Word frequency and reading comprehension. *Journal of Educational Research,* 1974, *67,* 259–262.

MARROU, H. I. *A history of education in antiquity* (trans. George Lamb). New York: Sheed and Ward, 1956.

MOESER, S. D., & BREGMAN, A. S. Imagery and language acquisition. *Journal of Verbal Learning and Verbal Behavior,* 1973, *23,* 91–98.

ONG, W. J. *Ramus: Method and the decay of dialogue.* Cambridge: Harvard University Press, 1958.

ONG, W. J. *The presence of the word.* New Haven: Yale University Press, 1967.

ONG, W. J. (ed.). *Knowledge and the future of man.* New York: Holt, Rinehart and Winston, 1968.

ONG, W. J. *Rhetoric, romance, and technology.* Ithaca, N.Y.: Cornell University Press, 1971.

PAIVIO, A. *Imagery and verbal processes.* New York: Holt, Rinehart and Winston, 1971.

QUINTILIAN. *Institutio oratoria* (trans. H. E. Butler). New York: Putnam's, Loeb Classical Library. 1921.

SINGER, D. W. *Giordano Bruno: His life and thought.* New York: Schuman, 1950.

TURNBULL, C. *Giordano Bruno.* San Diego: Gnostic Press, 1913.

WITTROCK, M. C. Response mode in the programming of kinetic molecular theory concepts. *Journal of Educational Psychology*, 1963, *54*, 89–93.

WITTROCK, M. C. Replacement and non-replacement strategies in children's problem solving. *Journal of Educational Psychology*, 1967, *58*, 69–74.

WITTROCK, M. C., Learning as a generative process. *Educational Psychologist*, 1974, *11*, 87–95.

WITTROCK, M. C., & CARTER, J. F. Generative processing of hierarchically organized words. *American Journal of Psychology*, 1975, *88*, 489–501.

WITTROCK, M. C.; DOCTOROW, M. J.; & MARKS, C. B. Reading as a generative process. *Journal of Educational Psychology*, 1975, *67*, 484–489.

WITTROCK, M. C., & GOLDBERG, S. M. Imagery and meaningfulness in free recall: Word attributes and instructional sets. *Journal of General Psychology*, 1975, *92*, 137–151.

YARMEY, A. D., & BOWER, N. V. The role of imagery in incidental learning of educable retarded and normal children. *Journal of Experimental Child Psychology*, 1972, *14*, 303–312.

YATES, F. *Giordano Bruno and the Hermetic tradition*. Chicago: University of Chicago Press, 1964.

YATES, F. *The art of memory*. London: Routledge and Kegan Paul, 1966.

ZAIDEL, D., & SPERRY, R. W. Memory impairment after commissurotomy in man. *Brain*, 1974, *97*, 263–272.

Glossary

by Konrad Talbot

Acetylcholine A chemical, specifically a quaternary ammonium compound, which serves as the neurotransmitter of motor neurons innervating skeletal muscles, as well as of various neurons in the autonomic nervous system, basal ganglia, limbic system, and perhaps the cerebral cortex.

Action potential (Spike, Impulse) A transient, excitatory change in the electrical state of a neuronal, usually axonal, membrane reflected in a "jump" in the voltage across the membrane from negative to positive values (see Fig. 1.6, pp. 22-23). This stimulus-induced electrical change occurring at one point along an axon generates another action potential in the succeeding (i.e., more distal) unmyelinated portion of the nerve fiber, leading to propagation of impulses down the axon.

Activation   The process by which brainstem systems induce arousal, either over prolonged periods (tonic activation) or for very short periods (phase activation).

Adaptation   Evolution or development of form and function appropriate to the environmental niche.

Affect   Emotional feeling or experience.

Amphetamines   The various chemical forms of amphetamine (principally Benzedrine, Dexedrine and Methedrine). These drugs are powerful central and sympathetic nervous system stimulants, markedly enhancing behavioral and electro-encephalographic (EEG) arousal, heart rate, blood pressure, and respiration. These effects are attributed to the ability of the amphetamines to enhance catecholamine neurotransmission by (1) causing the release of dopamine and norepinephrine from axon terminals, and at progressively higher doses, (2) inhibiting the breakdown of catecholamines and (3) stimulating dopamine and norepinephrine receptors (i.e., mimicking catecholamine neurotransmitters).

Analgesics   Drugs that reduce an individual's perception of pain.

Angiotensin   A hormone produced by the kidney in response to decreased blood pressure which, in a chemical form known as angiotensin II, is very effective in raising blood pressure and inducing drinking.

Anterior/posterior   Opposite directions along an axis in space which are used to describe the relative position of body, especially nervous system, structures. In a mammal which stands on all four limbs (e.g., rat, cat, dog, horse), anterior (or *rostral*) means "toward the face" and posterior (or *caudal*) indicates "toward the buttocks." These terms are differently defined for animals which stand on two limbs (i.e., humans): in the forebrain, anterior means "toward the face" and posterior indicates "toward the back of the head"; in the rest of the nervous system, the former term means "toward the top of," and the latter term "away from the top of," the head. It is important to realize that anterior and posterior are *relative* terms, so that structure A may be anterior to structure B, but posterior to structure C.

Antidiuretic hormone (ADH) A hormone produced by the hypothalamus, but stored by and released from the posterior pituitary gland, which acts upon the kidneys to decrease the amount of water excreted in the urine and thus conserve body water. The secretion of this hormone into the blood thus prevents diuresis (increased excretion of urine). As expected, dehydration of the body stimulates ADH release.

Aphasia Any of several central nervous system disorders affecting either speech production or comprehension.

Arousal A physiological state characterized by behavioral alertness, sympathetic predominance in the autonomic nervous system, and, most often, desynchronized electroencephalographic (EEG) activity.

Assay A procedure for measuring or determining the presence and quantity of a substance in a specimen.

Association zones or areas of the cerebral cortex All those regions of the cerebral cortex which are neither sensory nor motor in function.

Asymmetry (hemispheric) Used with reference to structural or functional differences between the right and left cerebral hemispheres.

Audition The sense of hearing.

Auditory Pertaining to the sense of hearing.

Autonomic nervous system (ANS) A subdivision of the nervous system which is to some extent independent or autonomous of the central nervous system and hence not readily under voluntary control. The ANS, which consists of the sympathetic and parasympathetic nervous systems, is involved in regulating visceral functions such as breathing, heart rate, blood pressure, intestinal movements, and hormone secretions. Also known as the *visceral* or "vegetative" nervous system.

Axon   The major type of communicating link between neurons: a neuronal process carrying (conducting) electrical impulses (spikes, action potentials) away from the cell body of one neuron to some portion of another neuron; a neuronal output channel. Also known as a nerve fiber.

Barbiturates   Drugs, such as nembutal, pentothal, and phenobarbital, belonging to a class of chemicals called "central nervous system depressants." The barbiturates are best known for their minor tranquilizing, antianxiety, and general anesthetic effects. Such effects are primarily due to the sedative-hypnotic properties of the drugs: their ability to induce, at successively higher doses (1) mental and muscular relaxation, (2) drowsiness, and (3) sleep. These effects are, in turn, the result of barbiturate-induced depression of recticular formation output.

Bilateral symmetry   The term commonly used to indicate that the right and left halves of the nervous system *appear* to be mirror images of one another in both structure and function. Detailed study of the right and left cerebral hemispheres reveals, however, differences or asymmetries between these brain structures in both physical and functional characteristics.

Biofeedback   Any of a class of methods employed in the operant or instrumental conditioning of bodily functions involving direct measurement of the momentary state of physiological processes as the response to be regulated.

Blood-brain barrier   The barrier preventing the passage of various substances, especially large molecules, from the blood system into the central nervous system. This protective shield unique to the brain and spinal cord is primarily the result of degradative enzymes in, and close appositions (tight junctions) between, cells (endothelia) forming the inner walls of central nervous system capillaries. Nevertheless, the expansions of glial cell processes covering these capillaries may also contribute to the blood-brain barrier, albeit to a lesser extent.

Brainstem That lower portion of the brain, consisting of the midbrain, pons, and medulla, which remains after removal of the forebrain and cerebellum. This complex region of the central nervous system includes, among numerous other structures (1) tracts carrying sensory information from skin, muscles, joints, cornea, ears, and mouth to forebrain areas, notably the thalamus, (2) axon bundles conveying motor commands from the cerebral cortex to motor centers in the brainstem and spinal cord, (3) raphé nuclei (implicated in regulation of sleep cycles), 4) reticular formation (critical in the control of arousal and gross bodily muscle tone), and (5) cardiac and respiratory centers.

Broca's area An area in the human frontal cortex of the left hemisphere that has been closely related to both syntactic and phonemic aspects of language function.

Cardiovascular system The heart and its network of blood vessels. This system is responsible for carrying basic nutrients, oxygen, water, and hormones to body cells and for conveying the metabolic waste products of those cells to the kidneys from which such products enter the urine.

Catecholamine (CA) A generic term for chemicals containing a *catechol* nucleus (a benzene ring with two adjacent hydroxyl groups) and a side chain ending with an amine (nitrogen-containing) group. Dopamine (DA) and norepinephrine (NE), both catecholamines, act as neurotransmitters in the central and peripheral nervous systems.

Central nervous system The brain and spinal cord.

Cerebellum   A large, highly convoluted structure immediately behind the brainstem, with which it is intimately connected. It appears to play an important role in maintaining postural symmetry between right and left halves of the body and co-ordinating movements.

Cerebral cortex   The multilayered tissue forming the outer surface of the forebrain. It is a portion of this tissue, specifically the neocortex, which has undergone the greatest proportional increase in the evolution of the mammalian brain. The neocortex is believed to be critically involved in cognitive functions.

Cerebral hemispheres   The outermost portion of the forebrain, consisting essentially of what is called the telencephalon (cerebral cortex, corpus callosum, basal ganglia, and limbic system: see **Forebrain** for functional description of these structures). Because the various parts of the telencephalon, which together comprise an appreciable portion of the forebrain, are each found clearly separated from one another on both right and left sides of the brain, each half (right and left) of the telencephalon is called a cerebral hemisphere.

Cetacea   Marine mammals, including dolphins, porpoises, and whales. Structurally, the brains of these animals appear as highly developed as that of man (e.g., relatively very high brain/body ratio and intricate pattern of cerebral convolutions).

Cochlea   A complex, coiled structure containing the sensory receptors for sound and located in the inner portion of the ear.

Cognitive processes   Higher psychological processes, such as perception, thinking, and reasoning.

Commissure   A compact bundle of axons lying parallel to one another which originate from neuronal cell bodies in a structure on one side (right or left) of the central nervous system and terminate (synapse) in large part in the same (homolateral) structure on the other side of the brain or spinal cord. Commissures, including the corpus callosum, are "two-way streets," carrying axons from right to left and from left to right sites in the central nervous system, allowing the two halves of that system to communicate directly with each other.

Commissurotomy The sectioning of the corpus callosum and the anterior commissure of the forebrain.

Convolution (cerebral) Infolding or wrinkling of the cerebral cortex. In the course of evolution, such infolding of tissue allowed a large increase in the surface area of the cerebral cortex without considerable expansion of cranial volume. Cerebral convolutions are very prominent in cetacea and primates.

Corpus callosum A massive, compact bundle of axons connecting the right and left cerebral cortices. The neuron from which an axon in this bundle derives is always located in the half of the cerebral cortex opposite (e.g., right) to that in which the axon terminates (e.g., left). The corpus callosum thus allows the two halves of the cerebral cortex to communicate directly with one another.

Correlates With respect to the neurosciences, usually a biological event that changes as behavior changes.

Cortex See **Cerebral cortex.**

Corticalized function Behavior function controlled by the cerebral cortex.

Cytoplasm The aqueous colloidal matrix of organic (e.g., proteins and lipids) and inorganic (e.g., water and simple salts) substances in which the various organelles (e.g., mitochondria, Golgi bodies, and endoplasmic reticulum) of a cell outside the nucleus are embedded. The protoplasm of a cell consists of its cytoplasm and a similar colloidal substance permeating, and in large part composing, the nucleus of the cell. Some, however, consider cytoplasm to include both the colloidal matrix and embedded organelles and the protoplasm to include all of the cell within its limiting membrane.

Decrementing   Reducing in quantity or amplitude.

Dendrites   The branched protrusions emanating from a neuron cell body toward which they convey information received from other neurons.

Dendritic tree   The entire grouping of branched dendrites that forms a treelike structure for a particular neuron.

Desynchrony   With respect to the electroencephalogram (EEG), low amplitude, fast activity, presumably reflecting independence in the activity in the populations of neurons giving rise to the EEG.

Dichotic listening   Listening to different auditory signals in each of the two ears.

Dopamine (DA)   A chemical, specifically a catecholamine, acting as the neurotransmitter of neurons found in the brainstem and the hypothalamus which innervate the hypothalamus, basal ganglia, limbic system, and cerebral cortex.

Ducted glands   See **Exocrine (ducted) glands**

Dyslexia   A central nervous system disorder in which the comprehension of written language (i.e. reading) is impaired.

Electrical potential   See **Potential (electrical)**

Electroencephalogram (EEG)   The pattern of electrical activity that may be recorded from the cerebral cortex using electrodes placed on the surface of the scalp.

Encephalization   The evolutionary increase in relative size and importance of the brain, particularly the forebrain, compared with other areas of the nervous system.

Endocast   Mold or cast made from the interior of a skull cavity which is used to obtain an idea of the shape and size of the brain.

Endocrine (ductless) gland Nonneural secretory tissue which, unlike exocrine or ducted glands, utilizes blood vessels and perhaps the lymph system to carry its secretions (hormones) to their target area of action. Among these are the pituitary, thyroid, and adrenal glands. Via their hormonal output, endocrine glands affect the central nervous system, and via hypothalamic control of the pituitary gland, the central nervous system affects the endocrine glands.

Engram A hypothetical construct for the physical basis of memory; a memory trace.

Environmental niche The totality of environmental factors (climate, food, water, enemies, etc.) normal to the life of a species.

Exocrine (ducted) gland Nonneural secretory tissue which, unlike endocrine or ductless glands, utilizes one (or more) special channels or ducts, rather than blood vessels, to carry its secretions (bathing fluids and/or enzymes) to their target area of action. Among these tissues are salivary, lacrimal (tear), and sweat glands.

Fixed-action pattern A complex behavioral response that, once initiated, always is executed in exactly the same manner, hence "fixed" regardless of intervening environmental events.

Forebrain (prosencephalon) The highest and most prominent portion of the brain which has undergone the greatest evolutionary expansion of any nervous system region. The major subdivisions of the forebrain are: (1) cerebral cortex (critically involved in cognitive functions), (2) basal ganglia (motor system modulator), (3) limbic system (subserving emotional and sexual behavior, as well as implicated in mediation of memory processes), (4) thalamus (relaying sensory, motor and limbic information to the cerebral cortex and basal ganglia), and (5) hypothalamus (critically involved in the control or modulation of numerous basic behaviors such as eating, drinking, sleeping, sexual activity, aggression, etc., as well as bodily temperature and hormone regulation).

Frontal lobe   The most anterior lobe of the cerebral cortex encased in large part by the forehead and temples. This region contains the motor area of the cerebral cortex.

Generative processing   In learning, cognitive processing that involves the active construction of meaning for stimuli.

Glia   A type of cell found in the nervous system which far outnumbers neurons. These cells, which unlike neurons do not generate spikes or action potentials, do myelinate axons, phagocytize dead neurons, guide the regrowth of axons in some parts of the nervous system, and perhaps regulate neurotransmitter storage and release. Glia may also play a role in maintaining the blood-brain barrier.

Gonads   The primary sex glands, ovaries in females and testes in males. These glands are responsible not only for producing the gamete cells (eggs in females and sperm in males) necessary in reproduction, but hormones (estrogens in females and androgens in males) which determine sex-dependent characteristics.

Gyrus (pl. gyri)   A distinct outfolding or tissue expansion between sulci in the mammalian cerebral cortex. The complex gyral pattern, which constitutes an obvious distinguishing feature of cetacean and primate brains, is quite variable from person to person.

Higher brain functions   General term used with reference to the activity of evolutionarily more recent brain structures, particularly the cerebral cortex.

Holistic   With reference to cognitive functions, the simultaneous processing of a configuration of information, rather than the sequential processing of its separate parts.

Homeostasis   In physiology, a steady, optimal state of the body, which an organism maintains through feedback-controlled biological activities known as homeostatic processes.

Hominoid/Hominid   Two subgroups of the most highly evolved primates. Hominoid refers to members of both subgroups: *Pongidae* (apes) and *Hominidae* (modern man and his man-like ancestors). Hominid refers only to members of the family *Hominidae* and thus to modern and primitive man, but not to apes.

Hypothalamus   A complex structure located at the base of the forebrain, immediately below the thalamus. This area, which is composed of many different collections of neurons (nuclei), is in direct contact with the master endocrine gland (pituitary) via neural and vascular connections. Through its reciprocal relationships with the endocrine system, limbic system, and brainstem, the hypothalamus is involved in modulating such basic behaviors as eating, drinking, sleeping, sexual activity, and aggression, in addition to controlling body temperature and hormone secretions.

Impulse   See **Action potential.**

Innervation   The termination of an axon or axons within a structure, specifically nervous system tissue, muscles, organs, glands, and blood vessels. To say that one area of the nervous system innervates a structure or tissue is to say that the axons originating in that area end (synapse) in the structure. If those same axons form a tract or nerve, we may also say the tract or nerve innervates the tissue.

Interocular   Between the eyes, particularly with reference to the distance between the eyes. In the course of vertebrate evolution, there has been a progressive decrease in interocular distance, resulting initially in partial and later in more complete overlap of the visual fields viewed by the two eyes. Such overlap allows for binocular vision, which is an important aid in accurately perceiving depth.

Invertebrate   An animal which, even when mature, lacks a backbone or spinal column. Included among the invertebrates are an enormous range of animals, for example: unicellular organisms (e.g., amoeba, planaria), coelenterates (e.g., hydras, sea anemones), molluscs (e.g., snails, squids, octopuses), and arthropods (e.g., crabs, lobsters, spiders, and insects). The different types and absolute number of invertebrates far exceed those of vertebrates.

Ions   Atoms or molecules (small or large) which bear an electrical charge.

Kinesthesis   See **Proprioception.**

Lateralization (hemispheric)   The differentiation of the two cerebral hemispheres with respect to function.

Learning   Processes leading to a relatively permanent change in behavior resulting from practice.

Lesion   As a verb, the process of damaging bodily tissue by cutting, heating, applying toxic substances, etc. As a noun, a focal area of tissue damage (i.e., a bodily area which has been lesioned).

Limbic system   An interconnected set of forebrain structures, including the amygdala, septum, hippocampus, and the cingulate cortex. The system both receives inputs from and directs outputs to the thalamus, hypothalamus, and brainstem. Similar to the hypothalamus, limbic system structures modulate motivational (e.g., eating and drinking), emotional (e.g., aggression), and sexual behavior. In addition, the hippocampus has been implicated in memory mechanisms.

Lobes of cerebral cortex   The major structural divisions of the cerebral cortex visible to the naked eye, differentiated primarily by prominent cerebral convolutions. These consist of the frontal, parietal, occipital, temporal, central (insula), and limbic lobes.

Locus coeruleus (Locus caeruleus, Locus ceruleus) A small nucleus located in the upper portion of a brainstem subdivision known as the pons. Axons of the locus coeruleus, which utilize norephinephrine (noradrenaline) as a neurotransmitter, innervate the spinal cord, raphe nuclei, cerebellum, hypothalamus, thalamus, limbic system, and cerebral cortex. Sources of input to the nucleus are the raphe nuclei, hypothalamus, anterior portions of the limbic system, and perhaps the cerebellum. The functions of the locus coeruleus remain obscure: although it has been proposed to play a role in dreaming and brain mechanisms of reward, there is now considerable doubt that the nucleus is involved in those activities.

Long-term memory Relatively permanent memory.

Metabolic processes Normal chemical transformations occurring within living cells which serve synthetic (e.g., protein production) and/or degradative (e.g., neurotransmitter inactivation) functions often directly or indirectly vital to the optimal maintenance of those cells.

Midbrain (mesencephalon) Uppermost portion of the brainstem containing primarily (1) tracts carrying sensory information from skin, muscles, joints, cornea, ear, and mouth to forebrain areas, notably the thalamus, (2) axon bundles conveying commands from the cerebral cortex to motor centers of the midbrain (superior colliculus, oculomotor nucleus, and red nucleus), (3) mesencephalic raphé nuclei (implicated in regulation of sleep cycles), (4) midbrain reticular formation (critical in the control of arousal and gross bodily muscle tone), and (5) four prominent collections of neurons (superior colliculus, oculomotor nucleus, red nucleus, and substantia nigra). Except for the superior colliculus, which is a sensory-motor integration center, virtually all the prominent nuclei of the midbrain control or modulate motor movement.

Mnemonic   A mental device or exercise that can be used to help one better remember something; a memory aid.

Modality   Any of the major types of sensation, such as vision, hearing, and touch.

Monotonic function   A mathematical function relating two variables in which increases in one variable always result in either increases or decreases in the second variable, but never both.

Morphology   The form and structure of organisms and their constituent tissues (e.g., organs and glands).

Motor neuron (motoneuron)   Neuron that controls muscle movement in some portion of the body. Lower motoneurons innervate muscle tissue directly. Upper motoneurons, as in the motor cortex, control movement by directly and indirectly innervating lower motoneurons.

Motor skills   Complex learned behaviors requiring muscular coordination.

Motor zones or areas of the cerebral cortex   Regions of the cerebral cortex the electrical activities of which initiate voluntary, and modulate involuntary, motor movements. These areas are found in the frontal lobe.

Myelin sheath   The fatty substance partially covering some axons. Myelin serves to increase the speed with which spikes or action potentials travel along nerve fibers.

Myelinization   The process by which a myelin sheath forms about an axon or collection of axons.

Narcotics   In medicine, a class of often addictive drugs derived from opium (e.g., heroin and morphine) which have potent analgesic and sedative actions; also known as narcotic analgesics. In law, a broader class of drugs, not necessarily addictive, which have morphinelike activity.

Natural selection   An evolutionary process in which individuals best adapted to an environment are most likely to survive and reproduce.

Nature-nurture interaction   The complex interplay of genetic predisposition and environmental influences in development and behavior.

Nerve   See **Tract.**

Neuroblast   The embryological cell type which differentiates into a neuron in the course of prenatal development.

Neuron   The nerve cell; the basic functional unit of the nervous system. The nervous system is composed in large part of neurons and another type of cell known as glia.

Neuroscience   The multidisciplinary study of the structure, chemical composition, and function (biological and behavioral) of the nervous system.

Neurotransmitter   A chemical substance released by a neuron's axon terminal or endfoot which diffuses across the synaptic gap to influence the electrical activity of the receiving neuron. Often abbreviated as transmitter.

Norepinephrine (NE), Noradrenaline (NA)   A chemical, specifically a catecholamine, which serves as the neurotransmitter of neurons found in the brainstem, including the locus coeruleus, the axons of which innervate the spinal cord, raphé nuclei, cerebellum, hypothalamus, thalamus, limbic system, and cerebral cortex. Some neurons in the sympathetic nervous system also utilize NE as a neurotransmitter.

Nucleus   In neuroanatomy, a collection of neuronal cell bodies in the central nervous system. Such a collection of neuronal tissue outside the central nervous system is referred to as a ganglion.

Occipital lobe   The lobe of the cerebral cortex directly behind the parietal and temporal lobes and adjacent to the skull along the lower, back portion of the head. This region consists largely of the area of the cerebral cortex most directly in receipt of visual (light) information.

Olfactory   Pertaining to the sense of smell.

Ontogeny   Refers to the growth and development of an individual organism as opposed to the evolutionary development of a species.

Operant conditioning   The strengthening of a response by reinforcing its occurrence.

Optic chiasm   The tissue mass formed by the crossing of the optic nerves in their paths from the eyes to their sites of termination in the thalamus and midbrain. Each optic nerve derives from the retinal ganglion cells of one eye.

Osmoreceptor   Sensory receptor sensitive to an increase in the osmolarity (particle concentration) of the solution bathing body cells (extracellular fluid) and hence responsive to dehydration of the body. Such receptors, found in the anterior portion of the hypothalamus, are specifically sensitive to a decrease in their own fluid content (intracellular fluid volume) resulting from an increased osmolarity of the immediately surrounding extracellular fluid. When electrically activated by such a drop in intracellular fluid volume, osmoreceptors trigger the release of antidiuretic hormone (ADH) from the pituitary gland.

Paired-associate task   A type of learning tool in which the learner is presented with pairs of items and later required to recall or recognize the second member of the pair when presented with the first.

Parameter   A number that provides specific values for a general equation.

Parasympathetic (division)   One of the two subdivisions of the autonomic nervous system, which increases its activity during periods of rest

Parietal lobe   The cerebral cortical lobe directly behind the frontal lobe and immediately above the posterior end of the temporal lobe. This region contains the area of the cerebral cortex most directly in receipt of sensory information from the skin and muscles: touch, pressure, position sense, etc.

Peripheral nervous system   All portions of the nervous system except the brain and spinal cord.

Phasic activation   Transient behavioral or electroencephalographic (EEG) increases in arousal that are relatively independent of the tonic activation level.

Phenylalanine   A chemical, specifically an amino acid, which is normally converted to tyrosine in various organs (principally the liver) and then transformed into dopamine or norepinephrine through several metabolic steps in certain neurons of the brain and sympathetic nervous system. Phenylalanine is thus a precursor of catecholamine neurotransmitters. It is a genetically linked inability to convert this compound to tyrosine which leads to the condition known as phenylketonuria (PKU), the most common of the inborn errors of metabolism that seriously threaten brain function.

Phonemes   The smallest units of sound in a language that serve to distinguish one utterance from another.

Phylogeny   Refers to the evolutionary history of species as opposed to the growth of a single organism (ontogeny) with which it is often contrasted.

Pituitary gland   The master endocrine gland controlling the release of hormones from other endocrine glands. Located just beneath the hypothalamus, with which it is connected via neural and vascular tissue, the pituitary gland is controlled by this brain structure and hormones released by other endocrine glands. Since the hypothalamus is also influenced by those hormones, the pituitary is to a large extent regulated by both direct and indirect feedback systems, both of which are inhibitory in nature.

Posterior. See **Anterior.**

Potential (electrical)   A difference in voltage between two points.

Preadaptation   Evolution of form or function in one niche that enables a species to enter and survive successfully in a different niche.

Primates   The order of mammals to which man, apes, and monkeys belong.

Processes (neuronal)   Relatively slender, prominent extensions or protrusions of membrane-bound cytoplasmic material and organelles from the cell body of a neuron. Depending on the function of such extensions, they are called either dendrites or axons.

Proprioception   The sense of position and movement of the limbs, dependent upon sensory receptors in skeletal muscles, joints, and/or tendons; also known as kinesthesis.

Psychotomimetics   Drugs which mimic psychosis by exerting a powerful effect on awareness and perception. Examples include mescaline and LSD. Some are similar in chemical structure to certain neurotransmitters.

Pupil   The opening in the iris of the eye which admits light.

Pupillometric   Refers to the measurement of pupillary diameter.

Raphé nuclei   A series of approximately eight nuclei located at the core of the brainstem. Surrounded by the reticular formation in nearly all cases, different raphé nuclei are found in each subdivision of the brainstem. The function of these brainstem structures is still unclear, but evidence exists to suggest a role for the raphé nuclei in pain and sleep mechanisms, as well as in sensing changes in body temperature and blood pressure.

Receptor (neurotransmitter)   A specialized area of a neuron to which a neurotransmitter binds and thereby influences the electrical state of that neuron.

Receptor (sensory)   A cell or neuronal process of a sensory system (e.g., visual or auditory) in which occur the first electrical responses to presentation of a sensory stimulus (e.g., light or sound), i.e., those structures responsible for converting (transducing) sensory information into neuronal electrical information. Examples of sensory receptor cells are the rods and cones in the eye and hair cells in the ear.

Reflexive behavior   Simple, automatic responses to highly specified environmental stimuli or triggers; not voluntary or spontaneous.

Resource-limited   In capacity models of attention, a cognitive process is resource-limited if insufficient capacity is available for optimal functioning, as when capacity is simultaneously allocated to another competing cognitive process.

Reticular formation   A diffusely organized reticulum or net of neurons occupying much of the core of the brainstem. The ascending axons of this neuronal system, terminating primarily in the thalamus, control arousal as indicated behaviorally or in the electroencephalogram (EEG).

Ribonucleic acid (RNA)   A large biological molecule composed of two long, intertwining strands of phosphate and sugar (ribose) compounds (i.e., phosphate-sugar-phosphate-sugar, etc.) linked via purine and pyridine bridges. RNA is critical in translating the genetic information contained in DNA molecules into the enzymes essential to metabolic processes.

Section   As a noun, this refers to a slice of tissue cut from a portion of the body. Since there are three planes in space, there are three standard types of sections: horizontal and two kinds of vertical slices (frontal or coronal cuts running along a line between the two ears and sagittal cuts running along a line from the face to the back of the head). Each of these types of sections is perpendicular to the others. As a verb, *section* refers to the actual cutting or slicing of tissue, usually into horizontal, frontal, or sagittal sections.

Semantic Referring to aspects of language at the level of meaning.

Semicircular canals A set of three roughly circular tubes oriented perpendicularly to each other, filled with a viscous fluid, and containing the receptor cells of the vestibular system. As such, the semicircular canals subserve the senses of head and body position and acceleration.The cochlea and the semicircular canals together comprise the inner ear.

Sensory zones or areas of cerebral cortex Regions of the cerebral cortex in relatively direct receipt of sensory information. There are separate sensory areas of the cerebral cortex for each of the various sensory systems (e.g., visual and auditory).

Serotonin A chemical, specifically an indoleamine, which acts as a neurotransmitter of neurons in the brainstem raphé nuclei, the axons of which innervate the cerebral cortex, limbic system, basal ganglia, thalamus, hypothalamus, substantia nigra, locus coeruleus, and spinal cord.

Short-term memory A limited-capacity memory system that retains recently acquired information for relatively brief periods of time.

Spike See **Action potential.**

Spike threshold (action potential threshold, critical firing potential) The degree of excitation (i.e., positive-going voltage change or depolarization) necessary to trigger an action potential in a neuronal membrane. This threshold varies for the different parts of the neuron: it is lowest for the axon and highest for the cell body and dendrites.

Spinal cord The long, complexly organized structure extending down the length of the neck and much of the back within a bony encasement known as the vertebral column. This structure (1) contains the cell bodies of neurons (spinal motor neurons) the axons of which innervate skeletal muscles, (2) receives and conveys sensory information from the skin, joints, and tendons to spinal motor neurons (thus allowing spinal reflexes, such as the knee jerk) and to the brain, (3) contains cell bodies of autonomic nervous system neurons, and (4) contains axons of nerve cells in the brain which control spinal motor neurons.

Splenium   The large posterior expansion of the corpus callosum through which the visual and auditory areas in one-half of the cerebral cortex communicate directly with the visual and auditory areas in the other half of the cerebral cortex, respectively.

Stereognostic   Referring to the perception of shapes by means of touch.

Stimulus   An environmental event that may be perceived by an organism.

Subcortical   Regions of the brain below the cerebral cortex.

Substantia nigra   A large midbrain nucleus, most neurons of which in primates contain the black pigment melanin. The axons of one portion of the substantia nigra (the *pars compacta*) terminate primarily in the basal ganglia and, to a lesser degree, in the cerebral cortex; the neurotransmitter of these nerve fibers is dopamine. Axons from the other major portion of the nucleus (the *pars reticulata*) innervate the thalamus and, to a lesser extent, the reticular formation and another midbrain area, the superior colliculus; the neurotransmitter of these nerve fibers is unknown. As to function, the substantia nigra has been implicated in regulation of motor movements, brain systems of reward, and memory mechanisms.

Sulcus (pl. sulci)   A distinct infolding or groove in the surface of the mammalian cerebral cortex. Especially prominent sulci are called fissures (e.g., Sylvian fissure). The large number and complicated pattern of sulci are an obvious distinguishing feature of cetacean and primate brains.

Sympathetic (division)   One of the two subdivisions of the autonomic nervous system (ANS) which increases its activity during times of stress and arousal—as distinguished from the parasympathetic subdivision of the ANS.

Synapse   The region of "communication" between the endfoot of one neuron and another neuron.

Synaptic gap   In a chemical synapse, the space between the endfoot of the "sending" neuron and the surface of the "receiving" neuron.

Synchrony   With respect to the electroencephalogram, high amplitude, slow activity, presumably reflecting transmembrane potentials occurring simultaneously in relatively large populations of neurons.

Tactual (tactile)   The sense of touch, one of a number of somatic (body) sensations.

Temporal lobe   The lowest-lying lobe of the cerebral cortex, located below the frontal and parietal lobes and adjacent to that portion of the skull just above the ears. This region contains the area of the cerebral cortex that receives auditory information most directly.

Termination (neuronal or axonal)   The ending(s) of an axon (or group of axons) as it (or they) contacts (synapses) upon a neuron.

Thalamus   Located at the "heart" or center of the forebrain, this large structure, which is composed of many different collections of neurons (nuclei), is important in relaying sensory, motor, and limbic information to the cerebral cortex and basal ganglia.

Tonic activation   The general level of arousal within the nervous system which usually changes rather slowly.

Tract   A compact collection of axons lying parallel to one another in the brain and/or spinal cord, which usually, but not always, have a common origin, destination, and/or function. A similar collection of axons outside the brain or spinal cord is called a nerve.

Transmembrane potential The difference in electrical charge (i.e., voltage) across the membrane of a cell.

Trauma A physical or psychological wound or injury.

Unilateral On one side only, as distinguished from bilateral, (i.e., on both sides).

Vertebrate An animal which, in its mature form, has a backbone, most often in the form of a segmented spinal column. This feature, as well as the frequent presence of a prominent internal skeleton, distinguishes vertebrates from invertebrates. Included among vertebrates are fish, amphibia (salamanders, frogs, and toads), reptiles (turtles, lizards, snakes, and crocodiles), birds, and mammals.

Vestibular system The network of sensory (semicircular canals) and neural (vestibular nerve, nuclei, and tracts) structures subserving two types of mechanosensation: (1) position of the head in space (gravity or equilibrium sense), and (2) intensity and direction of linear, and especially angular, acceleration of the head. The brain uses this information to determine the spatial orientation of the body as a whole and both quantitative and qualitative aspects of bodily acceleration.

Viscera Those organs within the body trunk (thorax and abdomen), including the heart, lungs, kidneys, liver, and intestines. The term has also been used to refer to all tissues within the body trunk: organs, glands, blood vessels, nerves, ganglia, and connective tissues.

Wernicke's area An area in the left cerebral hemisphere near the border between the temporal and parietal lobes, critical to language comprehension.

Index

Myelinization, 6
Myers, Ronald, 90, 91

Nachson, I., 115
Narcotics, 26
Natural selection, 41, 44
Nature-nurture interaction, 55
Neanderthal endocast, 45
Nebes, Robert D., 97-105, 120, 137*n*
Neisser, U., 117, 134
Neuroblasts, 16
Neurons, 5-6, 16-25; cortical, 5-6, 8-10, 43;
    direction of operation of, 17; electrical potential
    of, 20-23; feature extractors, 10, 27-28; learning
    and, 29-30; of lower animals, 17; measurement
    of activity of, 32, 34-35; membrane of, 19-21;
    motor, 6, 8, 14; nucleus, 10; number of, 16,
    46-47; prototype, 17-18; resting, 19, 20; retinal,
    51-52; sensory, 6, 9-10, 18; synapses of, 17,
    18, 19, 21-24, 29-30; synchronously active, 32;
    types of, 18
Neurosciences, 4
Neurotransmitters, 17-19, 20-25; excitatory, 21-23;
    identification of, 24; inhibitory, 21-25; release
    of, 17-18, 21-23
Newcombe, P., 120
Norepinephrine, 24-25
Norman, D. A., 66, 71
Nucleus, 10

Occipital lobe, 6, 7, 9
O'Hanlon, James, 79-81
Olfaction, 56; commissurotomy and, 93;
    evolution of, 52-54; split brain and, 91
Olfactory bulb, 15
Ong, Walter, 168*n*
Ontogenetic development, 16
Operant regulation of activation, 79-81
Opium, 26
Optic chiasm, 90
Optic fibers, 9
Ornstein, R. E., 105, 140
Osmoreceptors, 13
Ostrom, J. H., 48

Pain, perception of, 26
Paivio, A., 164, 168*n*, 170, 175
Pallie, W., 118
Papcun, G., 115
Parasympathetic nervous system, 14
Parietal lobe, 6-8
Parkinson's disease, 24
Parry, M. E., 75
Part-whole relationships, 102-103, 141
Payne, D. T., 75
Peters, R. P., 55
Petersen, I., 66
Phasic activation, 82
Phenylalanine, 24
Phonetic units, perception of, 111-112
Picton, T. W., 67
Piercy, M., 119
Pitch perception, 113

Pituitary, 7, 12-14
Polt, J. M., 74
Polyak, S., 52
Poppen, R., 119
Popper, Karl, 42
Poster, M. I., 67
Pratt, R., 120
Preadaptations, 46
Preliminary phenomenological schemes, 143
Primates, brain of, 5, 8, 43-44, 50, 56-57
Problem solving, pupillary dilation and, 74-76
Prioceptive information, 91
Propositionality, 138, 140
Prosimians, brain of, 50
Psychotomimetic drugs, 26
Pupillary dilation: attention and, 67-76;
    perceptual detection and, 69-70; perceptual
    discrimination and, 70; problem solving and,
    74-76; short-term memory and, 71-74
Pyramidal neuron, 18

Quintilian, 155

Radinsky, L., 40
Ramus, Peter, 166
Raphé nuclei, 25
Rasmussen, T., 108, 119
Ratcliff, G., 120
Rats, 8, 31
Ray, W., 121
Receptors, 8, 9, 19; density, 10; osmoreceptors, 13;
    stretch, 13; touch, 11, 32, 33
Rechtschaffen, A., 77
Reflexive behavior, 14
Regulation, 7
Remington, R., 115, 121
Renaissance, memory systems during, 162-166
Reproduction, 12
Reptiles, brain of, 15; evolution of, 51-52; size
    of, 42, 48
Resource-limited tasks, 71
Reticular formation, 7, 11-12, 32, 33
Retina, 9, 51, 53
Rhead, J., 147
Right cerebral hemisphere, 97-105; appositional
    cognition and, 138-141, 143; commissurotomy
    and, 91-96, 101, 102, 104; early studies of, 97-99;
    handedness and, 119-120; hemisphericity and,
    121-122; holistic bias and, 102-103; language
    processing in, 93-94, 103, 114, 117, 120, 123,
    139-140, 178; memory and, 101; mental
    function distribution studies and, 99-104;
    part-whole relationships and, 102-103, 141;
    perception and, 100, 101, 139; visual-spatial
    processing in, 92-95, 99-102, 121, 139, 140.
    See also Hemispheric specialization
Rizzolata, G., 108
RNA, 29
Robbins, K., 108
Rogers, L., 117-118
Russell, R., 108

Sait, P., 113
Satz, P., 120

DATE DUE